THE

HIDDEN PLACE

Connie Victoria Volk

DEDICATION

This book is dedicated to

The High King of Heaven and
Earth

And to my mother,

Erna Irene Ehrmann,

Who was always my biggest
encourager.

ACKNOWLEDGEMENTS

Special thanks to:

The welcoming members of the Wordsmiths who saw a diamond in the rough and helped me cut and polish it;

Gloria Kerzmann whose timely words of encouragement from start to finish were like sunshine in my heart;

Mary Thom who did the very first reading of this book;

Andra Marquardt for her photo of the author;

Mary Schmitz for her expertise in uploading the book;

Grace Bergan who so freely shared her expertise in the organization and arranging of the manuscript;

Carla Iszler who sowed a seed of faith and bought the first book when as yet there was none;

Stephanie Kuhn who was always an eager, engaged listener;

Valerie Kuhn who believed in me and believed in the book;

Jonathan Kuhn who brought me the inspiration for one of the final chapters;

My many dear friends who were a constant source of encouragement and

Dennis and Dr. Jen Clark for their book, *deep relief NOW*

TABLE OF CONTENTS

What do you do when you meet someone who "really loves Jesus" or who believes they really have had a "personal experience in His presence?" You might immediately try to caution (like most pastors) or divert to more "correct theologies." That can happen when folks become nervous or defensive in regard to enjoying a personal relationship with their Lord!

Connie Volk simply wants to share her experience with the Christ who met her in the "Hidden Place" and saved her by His great mercy and grace. She invites us vulnerably into her heart and into her questions as she sorts through the problems and struggles in her journey of faith. We aren't asked to debate or analyze her experience, just listen and enter in where we might.

Is it okay if a friend discovers and meets Jesus in a way quite different from me? Can I just allow myself to accept the invitation and walk with another believer who prays, "Forgive me, Christ Jesus. Help me to relax my will and open my heart's door!" In simple description, Connie sees the yoke of Christ "at rest on her shoulders, easy and free."

The Hidden Place is written in very brief vignettes and is full of Scripture to bring encouragement. Even when you wonder and question along the way, invite the Holy Spirit to stir your own heart and bring you closer to His!

Pastor Bob Nordvall

Chaplain at Heartview Foundation

Addiction Recovery, (Bismarck, ND)

Missionary to Estonia through EEMN

Former missionary to Papua, New Guinea

ENDORSEMENTS

I was caught up with the experiences Connie had; but, as I read, I too experienced His presence.

In the beginning I found myself envious of her encounters with the Lord. Then I realized I could enter in and believe as a child. To ask, receive, question, and hear His replies and to see His love is what I hope every reader would experience.

I read a story to the Healing Room Kids about a girl who had a tea party with Jesus. Jael was probably the age of eight when she heard it. She went home and asked her mom if she could have a tea party for Jesus. She explained that she set it up and had a pillow for Jesus to sit on. She waited, and He came! She said, "I saw His hair and eyes! It wasn't like this (pointing to me and her); it was with my eyes closed and in here (pointing to the side of her head)."

The young girl asked Jesus questions. One was, "When are you coming back?" She said He answered, "You'll have to wait and see." What seemed like hours was only ten to twenty minutes.

Connie's way of writing brings the ability to imagine with her, and the scripture references help the reader to be grounded in the Word. Her poetry brings such richness.

Moses wanted to see the manifest glory of God, and he desired to know that presence experientially. Jesus promised to show Himself to those who believe (John 14:21).

Connie showed God's character and His way of relating to her. She shared His love, mercy, grace and compassion. By sharing her intimate times with our Lord, she has taught us how we can respond, grow, and give God glory by having our characters resemble His!

Psalm 65:4 says, "Blessed is the man You choose, and cause to approach You, that he may dwell in Your courts. We shall be satisfied with the goodness of Your house, of Your holy temple."

This book was so tasty for me. I read it slowly, one bite at a time.

Lola Copenhaver
Intl. Assoc, of Healing Rooms, Region Five Dir.
Dir. of Healing Rooms of the Northern Plains
Dir. Of Healing Room Kids, Bismarck, ND

WHAT OTHERS ARE SAYING

"A journey of intimacy to blaze a trail for others who desire to live in His presence."
"Delightful, refreshing, like a drink of cool water."

Patti Nordvall

"This book is the Cadillac of devotionals. With beautiful prose the author brings the reader into her intimate journey with the Lord."

Gayle Larson Schuck, author

"Absorbing words of life. They are illuminated treasures that go to the depths of His presence in revelation."

Judy Pattengale

"These writings are so beautifully intimate. They stir me deeply. This is what the world longs for—whether they know it or not."

Susan Doppler

"This book was so tasty to me. I read it slowly, one bite at a time.
I could imagine with Connie while remaining grounded in the Word.
Her poetry brought such richness.
Come, enter also into His glory."

Lola Copenhaver
Intl. Assoc. of Healing Rooms, Region Five Dir.

INTRODUCTION

I have heard it said that when you read a book, you never know where it will take you. So it was with the writing of this book.

The Lord prompted me to begin writing on a Thursday morning exactly two weeks after my mother went home to be with Him. I felt empty, alone and without a purpose. The inspiration of this book became the perfect intersection of time with eternity. I finished most of the rough draft sixteen days later. There was an air of urgency about it. I did not delay.

I sat in expectation every morning to see what He would have to say. I was His ready scribe and was always surprised and touched by what came forth. It was a journey into the hidden place of the heart of God.

Every chapter contains treasures from the two central passages of Colossians 3:2-4 and Ephesians 3:14-20. I encourage you to begin and end each chapter with soaking in the living truth of these words until they are absorbed into your heart. They will anchor you in Him and in His love.

All scriptural references are taken from the Passion Translation unless otherwise noted. The harmony between that translation and this book will expand your revelation of all Who Jesus really is.

In the writing of this book, I often found prose proving inadequate to release the deep fountains of my heart. This sent me to seek refuge in the flow of poetry to give expression to these bubbling emotions. Therefore, I have used prose and verse to share my encounter. Each chapter starts and ends with poems. These are best experienced within the realm of your heart and of His Spirit.

I expose the deepest parts of my being, hoping that my vulnerability may help you find your own path into the presence of the living God.

The King is soon coming in the clouds for His bride, with whom He is utterly and totally in love. He longs for intimacy with us, not only in the future, but even now in the present.

May your journey to the hidden place be sparked with wonder and delight as you surrender to rest in the tender heart of God. May the passionate love of the heavenly Bridegroom become your very own.

SCRIPTURAL REFERENCES

Colossians 3: 2-4

"Yes, feast on all the treasures of the heavenly realm and fill your thoughts with heavenly realities, and not with the distractions of the natural realm.

Your crucifixion with Christ has severed the tie to this life, and now your true life is hidden away in God in Christ. And as Christ himself is seen for who he really is, who you really are will also be revealed, for you are now one with him in his glory!"

Ephesians 3: 14-20

"So I kneel humbly in awe before the Father of our Lord Jesus, the Messiah, the perfect Father of every father and child in heaven and on the earth. And I pray that he would unveil within you the unlimited riches of his glory and favor until supernatural strength floods your innermost being with his divine might and explosive power.

Then, by constantly using your faith, the life of Christ will be released deep inside you, and the resting place of his love will become the very source and root of your life.

Then you will be empowered to discover what every holy one experiences—the great magnitude of the astonishing love of Christ in all its dimensions. How deeply intimate and far-reaching is his love! How enduring and inclusive it is! Endless love beyond measurement that transcends our understanding—this extravagant love pours into you until you are filled to overflowing with the fullness of God!

Never doubt God's mighty power to work in you and accomplish all this. He will achieve infinitely more than your greatest request, your most unbelievable dream, and exceed your wildest imagination! He will outdo them all for his miraculous power constantly energizes you."

LOW

There is no category into which
life can be neatly placed.

No matter how hard we try to
bend and fit, move and place, it
defies all logic, sense and grace.

We poke and pout, pull and push,
twist and turn. We pick and kick,
shout and doubt, ponder and
wander.

Finally, we recognize that our
finite intellect has come up
against the grand design of a
mind and a will that is so much
greater than ours.

We realize then that the best
choice is to walk humbly with
our God (Micah 6:8 RSV), going
low in the face of powerful Love

who invites us into true life.
There we find that low is the way
to go.

Chapter 1

THE JOURNEY

The boat ride of life—
it flows in and out, to and fro...

over the sands of time
round the sharp turns of hurt
past the wired gates of hate
under the bridge of 'Too Late'
on the wild floods of love
near the green pastures of peace
and into the dock of The Rock.

Chapter 1

THE JOURNEY

The tiny stream of spring fed water sparkles in the sunlight. Its cool, gurgling flow draws me from my path. I watch in fascination as it hopscotches its way in delight over the pebbles on the sandy bottom. Wiping the noon day perspiration from my brow, I kneel, leaning forward for a taste of that thirst-quenching drink.

In that instant, I catch a glimpse of my reflection in the water. My thoughts flood backward in time to the outset of my journey fifty-two years ago. My name? Call me Everyone. Call me Anyone. This is your story. This is my story.

I began with no deliberate destination in mind. However, the farther I traveled, the more disillusioned I became with the lure of vain attractions on the fast-paced interstate of life. My once polished brown shoes had grown worn, dusty and ragged on that roadway. The embers of passion for living had become ashes on the floor of my heart, and yet there still lingered a desire, a longing, for something more. I found myself a stressed, weary human being with little strength remaining.

Within I wondered if there were yet new treasures to be discovered and if I could make it to the end.

In search of rest, I weaned myself away from the crowded thoroughfare and sought out the little-known byway of solitude. The deepest yearning of my heart had always been for peace. There were fellow travelers who encouraged me along the way; but, as of late, I was more so drawn into the solitude of the One Who Sees (Gen. 16:13 NIV).

With a shake of my head, I bring myself back to the present, cupping my hands to drink my fill of the refreshing water. It has such an unmistakable taste of life to it that I can't help but wonder if I am nearing the end of my search. With renewed energy and hope, I resume my trek.

This afternoon I am winding my way along a lonely, narrow pathway in the sunlit woods when a long-forgotten melody rises from deep within me. The words flow over my lips with ease. "I'm a poor wayfaring stranger, traveling through this world of woe…" My path becomes less frequented but more alive with the anticipation of an unknown adventure awaiting me.

As I continue through the stillness of the woods to a spacious clearing, my heart leaps with expectation. My eyes are treated to the most welcome appearance of a plain, white, thatched roof cottage. It has no definitive edges, but neither is it round. It is accented with beautiful, scented peonies, pink daylilies and an array of multi-colored roses. A winding slate walkway leads to the entrance.

It is so simple and inviting that I hasten forward to the rough-hewn wooden door. To my disappointment, it is locked. Standing there wondering what I should do next, I see a tall, willowy figure rounding the corner. He is dressed in a brown homespun frock with His face hidden in the shadow of the hood. His voice is kind. I feel no fear.

In slow deliberation He pulls an object from His deep pocket, placing it with love into my care. It is cool to the touch but seems to fit my hands as though being made just for them.

"This is a gift from the Ancient of Days (Dan. 7:9-10). It is the key of David, unlocking intimacy and prayer" (Rev. 3:7-8).

Puzzled, I watch His departure into the woods and then open my hands to reveal a long iron key with a heart shaped end (Rev. 3:7 footnote). My fleeting impression is that it had been forged in fiery flames ages ago. I know with certainty it will fit the keyhole in front of me. Just as I step forward to insert the key, a soft light begins streaming out through that lock. My heart races as I turn the antiquated key to unlock the heavy door. To my surprise, it swings open to the touch, almost as if someone were already on the other side pulling it open for me. Could the answer I've been seeking be waiting within?

As I step through the doorway, the eyes of my heart are illuminated by the light emanating from the Living One inside (Eph. 1:18). The epitome of all wisdom stands in flesh before me (Col. 2:3). His eyes are like flames of fire (Rev. 1:14), revealing the thoughts and motives of my heart with a glance (Heb. 4:12-13). I move my weight from one leg to another, shifting my eyes from Him to my surroundings. As I do, the entire physical scene before me expands in an ethereal metamorphosis. I realize this cottage is merely an outer shell of what lies beyond. To my utter amazement, I find myself within the luminous, living walls of the hidden place, the ultimate pearl of great price, the dwelling place of the King. I am now His guest, and I know I am about to be transformed.

Chapter 1

THE MYSTERY

I want to show you a mystery

great and true,

an open door for you

to peek through.

The colors are purple and blue,

A royal tapestry true

—it is My essence—

peeking through.

I look at you and see you

through and through.

I begin to change you through
and through

until when you look at you,

you see Me

peeking through.

Col. 1:26-27

Chapter 2

WHO WOULD HAVE THOUGHT

*From ashes to life—who would
have thought?*

Even in the death of dreams

All is not as it seems.

From the death of hopes

To the despair of the soul,

Keep your eyes on the goal.

*For there is a Creator, mighty
indeed*

You need only pray

To be shown His way.

Life springs up—hope is not dead.
Dreams come alive.
Again—into life we dive.

Chapter 2

THE HIDDEN PLACE

I stand still, just inside the doorway, my eyes staring at Him in wonder. Who really is this Being before me, beckoning for me to enter? I know, and yet I don't know. How does one who is mortal react to One who is immortal? In my astonishment words fail me, but I take advantage of His gracious offer of time to rest and clean up from my long, dusty journey. I turn to walk upstairs but can't help glancing backward to make sure this is all real and He is real.

Later, with a hint of hesitancy in my steps, I rejoin Him downstairs. A smile brightens His face as He invites me to join Him. He leads me through a vine covered trellis into a natural stone covered patio. Tall ferns surround the seating area. An eight-foot rock fountain fills the moist, fresh air with the soft music of flowing water.

"I want to tell you about this extraordinary place," the King shares as we make our way toward the brown wicker table and seats.

Taking my place across from Him, a feeling of home settles over me. I am able to relax as I note

that the flames of fire in His eyes now are veiled by
a deep tenderness shining through.

In a soft voice He begins. "Your yearning
for love forms an entrance into the heart of God.
My heart is a living entity–both a refuge for the
body and a realm of peace for the soul. This secret
place is hidden within Me," He continues, "and it is
hidden within you. There is no well-known path
leading here. It's often a journey of a lifetime with
many twists and turns—often testing you to your
limits, or so it seems."

With a rueful smile, I nod in agreement.

"Only those with a great hunger and thirst
will go through the effort to search it out. Once
found, a traveler will hold it close and treasure it as
the well spring of his life" (Eph. 3:17).

He speaks now with more intensity. "It's of
inestimable worth because I gave My life to
purchase your access to it, to Me. When you
unlocked that door and walked through, you severed
the tie to your old life (Col. 3:3). By faith you
allowed Me entrance into your heart just as I
allowed you entrance into Mine."

His voice resonates with the richness of
eternity. "I am the Way, the Truth and the Life
(John 14:6). As you humble yourself, you become
one with Me and receive as much of Me as you
desire. I am the fountain that never runs dry. I have
an inexhaustible supply of whatever you need. I am
your root of life for body, soul and spirit (John 1:4

footnote). You are created in My image to mirror Me, to be one with Me, to be in union with Me."

I am beginning to follow His line of thinking.

"Let not your thoughts be filled with the distractions of the natural realm," He cautions (Col. 3:2). "They will only serve to destroy the perfect peace and intimacy between us."

In deep concentration, I find that this is not at all like talking to another human being. This wisdom is not originating in His mind. It is surging up from a deep inner reservoir and just flowing over His lips. I feel like a pawn in a chess game, trying to understand the ways of the king on the board. But at the same time, I feel more valued than ever before in my life.

"Your true identity is in Me and so is your ultimate satisfaction. Live in Me–in the hidden place" (Ps. 91:9-10). He smiles. "I am the origin of all for which you long. In Me you will be completely and totally satisfied."

Leaning forward with pursed lips, I want to believe Him. Do I dare? Can I trust Him? I study His face but can find no trace of deception reflected in his eyes (Heb. 7:26). His words of truth latch onto my heart and cannot be denied.

Yes, my quest has led me to the right place. Tonight, I will sleep in peace.

Chapter 2

THE SOURCE

The pearl opens...

I see within it the Source of Love.

Its luminous glow is irresistibly
iridescent.

It draws one into itself.

It enfolds with gentleness.

It engulfs with wonder.

It enraptures with mystery.

It ravishes with love.

I am drawn in

to the Source...

to remain forever and ever.

Chapter 3

THE CIRCLE OF LIFE

The circle of life goes round and round

Where it begins cannot be found.

Oh, but it can.

Life began in the heart of God.

Death ended in the Son of God.

Life continues in the Spirit of God.

And so the circle of life goes round and round

And where it ends cannot be found.

Chapter 3

THE SHARING

I yawn and stretch in the warm morning sunlight beaming its way through the bedroom window. *I must have slept the night away on a featherbed of peace.* For the first time in years I'm looking forward to just being able to eat breakfast. I'm hungry. It's as though this is my first day of being fully alive.

I hurry downstairs to the aroma of French Vanilla coffee. My attentive Host leads me to a small oak table spread with freshly picked strawberries and raspberries. Warm blueberry muffins and condiments surround a bowl of boiled eggs.

I love the idea that we can sit face to face across from one another (Ps. 27:8). Leaning in to absorb His every word and expression, I regret that in my past brief times with Him, I had done most of the talking. Now I can't even think of anything to say. All my questions lie dormant in His presence.

"When you arrived here," He begins, "you had come to the end of yourself; but when you walked through the door of the hidden place, your true life began. Life in Me is a life that continues.

It's ever expanding. You will never come to the end of it because I fill time and eternity. That is why nothing will ever be able to separate you from My love which is overflowing. It's breadth, length and width are without measurement" (Eph. 3:18-19).

As I gaze into His eyes, I get the barest glimpse of what He is talking about. I can't take my eyes off His.

"I am not containable," He smiles. "You can't put Me in a bottle and study Me. That's why My Spirit is often described in terms such as wind, aroma and fire. That's also the reason you see countless hues and colors in the sunsets, sunrises and in the flames of a fire. They all speak of Me and My infinite glory.

Never before had I considered such a correlation. I sit amazed, no longer interested in the strawberry in my hand.

"I am speaking My heart to you right now. I am Wisdom Incarnate. I long to share with you more of Myself for you are part of Me. The more you know about Me, the more you will know of yourself" (Col. 3:4).

Glancing out the window at the rising morning sun, He muses, "You can spend a lifetime searching for your worth; but only when you find Me, will you find the treasure of you."

With sparkling eyes He reveals, "I have made you multifaceted—like a brilliant diamond. I see all the radiant light that can be reflected from you. You were created to mirror My light to the world—not to be concealed under a basket" (Matt. 5:14-16).

Feeling more and more at home in His presence, I remember to take a bite of the huge, now warm, strawberry between my fingers.

"Simply allow yourself to be who I created you to be. Here in the secret place, without fear, you can practice who you really are until you get comfortable with My original design for you. Your heart will take delight as you see the evidence of My work becoming visible on this earth through you" (Eph. 3:20).

My thoughts race with the possible scenarios of what He is suggesting. I'm also aware that He has just lit in the deepest recesses of my heart the same slow, steady flame that is mirrored in His eyes.

What can possibly lie ahead, I wonder. Where will my next step lead?

My future is no longer a dead end but an open door to endless possibilities.

Chapter 3

FREE

The swing below me
The wind over me
The sun on me
FREE...
Free to be...me.

Chapter 4

WHITE AS SNOW

White as snow, white as snow,

Wind of the Spirit, blow.

Wash our minds, cleanse our
hearts

So we never need to part,

Being one with you in all we do.

Chapter 4

THE SHEPHERD

I am startled into wakefulness the second morning by an unexpected knock on my bedroom door. I turn over in my antique brass bed to see the Shepherd standing just inside. His white garmented figure is framed in the early morning sunlight as He comes my way. A sense of security sweeps over me. I realize that throughout the night He has been in the darkened hallway, standing guard at my door (Ps.145:20).

He speaks and every word becomes an etching of gold written on my heart. "Your sins are forgiven."

The look of love and compassion in His eyes penetrates my heart, breaking into pieces the doors of bronze (Is.45:2) I had erected years ago to protect myself from any further betrayal. However, while those barriers had kept others out, they had also locked me in.

My heart cries out in wonder at the mere thought of freedom. *Could it be true? Could such a thing actually happen?*

The words echo deep within me. *Forgiven? Forgiven of what? I ask myself. There is so much. How much could be forgiven?*

"Everything," came His silent answer within me.

"Everything?" My eyes widen. "All my sins?"

"Yes, everything."

At once there comes a gushing forth of His river of forgiveness, and all the bars of iron are cut asunder (Is. 45:2). The power of unbelief, backed up by fear, is exposed in an instant and washed away in a wave of mercy. I am free inside. Nothing else matters. I am forgiven…the most precious words I have ever heard. Oh, the wonder and inexpressible joy of it all. His kindness has given me that for which I have hungered. He has presented me with more than what I could have ever asked; He has gifted me with the true longing of my heart (Ps. 145:13,18-19).

Warm tears of joy come streaming from my eyes. While lying on my back, I feel the wetness of them trickling into my ears.

In between sobs I manage to choke out the words, "The blood of Jesus…oh, thank You, Lord, for Your precious blood that makes all this possible" (1 Peter 1:18-19).

I look up to meet the eyes of the Shepherd, and I am drawn into the blazing fire coming to the forefront of His gaze. With an undeniable authority that shakes the remaining foundations of evil surrounding me, He commands, "Stand up. Pick up that veiled bed of codependency. Release it to Me and start to live again" (Mark 2:11-12).

His power begins surging through me. It feels as though all the empty reservoirs of hope, expectation and strength are being restored, and life is sweet again (Prov. 13:12). Now I have the faith to once more believe that with His explosive power I can tackle anything (Phil. 4:13). The mountains of gaining my Father's approval by doing all things in my own strength are brought low (Is. 40:4 RSV).

I find myself literally lifted to my feet by the strong hand of the Shepherd. In joy, my spirit also leaps in instant recognition of my true source of approval and identity…God Himself.

"I see now, Lord. I see the truth. I see who I am. I am the righteousness of God in Christ Jesus (II Cor. 5:21). I can walk in faith (II Cor. 5:7 RSV), and I can do all things through You who strengthens me" (Eph. 3:16-17).

My heart rejoices at the thought of it all. I came here to the hidden place with nothing of tangible worth, and now I have everything. I'm not only innocent; I am also free. I am flooded with such incredible grace. Like a river overflowing its banks, I am now full of faith and love for the Shepherd (I Tim. 1:14).

Chapter 4

THE YOKE

Your yoke is heavy—let it go.

Exchange with the Shepherd of
your soul.

His yoke is light—allow it to be

At rest on your shoulders, easy
and free.

Take no thought for the morrow,

Just flee to Me.

Release your sorrows

And all your debris.

His yoke is easy, His burden light

His smile on your face—oh, so bright.

His strength will hold you

His love enfold you.

Matt. 11:28-30 RSV

Chapter 5

MATCHING

Match my heart to Yours.
Fit together the pieces of the
puzzle so that
I may be one with You,
perfected,
fulfilled in You.

Let my heart beat in rhythm
with Yours,
gather its life and
receive its fruit from Yours.
Let my heart yield in submission
to Yours.

Let my heart match Yours.

Chapter 5

THE FIRE OF LOVE

The tiny fruit tarts tantalize my taste buds as I sit down with the Shepherd for a mid-afternoon snack. I relax, breathing in the sweet scent of peppermint tea warming my blue ceramic cup. As I lean back to listen, He begins to speak.

"I really enjoy having you here with me. You know that, don't you?"

He smiles in the brightest, most fun-filled way. I can't help but smile back at Him. His mere presence tinkles the joy bells of my heart.

My inquisitive mind is racing on a treadmill of questions.

"How do I find my way around here? Are there many different rooms and areas?"

"The hidden place is capable of unending expansion," He explains, "because it is hidden in Me (Col. 3:3). I am God! I hold the world in My hands. There is no limit to Me."

With the eagerness of a young boy, He volunteers, "You can explore for eternity and not come to the end. But I will show you what I believe will be your favorite spot."

He leads me to a room matching my mental image of the ideal setting for closeness—a dimly lit sitting room with small bouquets of scented roses, lavender and sweet peas scattered here and there. Soft harp music fills the air, and a plush ruby-red sofa welcomes us to lounge in front of a glowing fireplace. My imagination comes alive, just picturing myself there.

"It's here I will come to sit with you because I know this will be your secret hide-a-way for sharing. However, have no fear. No matter where you are, I will know and find you there. Everyone has his own idea of what that perfect place would be. That is why I am the God of the individual—not the crowd. I am personal, and I long to spark the fire of love in each of My own. I created you. I know you and everything of value that lies within. I love you."

My heart leaps at His words. How could I have ever doubted that such a Person exists?

The warmth of His sentiment causes me to respond in kind, "My love for You also, my King, is growing with each day. Teach me to be more like You. I came here a cracked, leaky vessel. Now allow Your light to shine through those cracks to light the way for others."

He smiles, takes my hand and leads me to the fireplace. It is here He fans into fire the flame in my heart. My world comes alive again, and my heart remembers how to sing, "I'm in love. I'm in

love. I'm in love." The words come dancing out of
my mouth and all creation joins with me.

Chapter 5

OUR LOVE FOR HIM
(Jesus' Perspective)

Your love for Me is deep…
It has a breath and a sweep.
Sing to Me…
Your love, let Me see.
It brings Me great joy,
Feeling like a young boy,
In love with life and you
For Your love rings, oh, so true.

Chapter 6

THE REALM WITHIN

There is a realm within that
exists unseen,

Found between

This earth below and the one
above,

Between the natural realm and
the realm of love.

Look deep inside and you will
find

A shift will move you into His
mind,

The mind of Christ. Who would
have thought

That His death for you all this
would have bought?

Your position in Christ you there
will take

And the grip of the enemy you
will break,

The grip of fear, of lack,

The grip of stress, the panic
attack.

The unseen realm is outside of
time.

The tick of the clock can't hold
you in line.

You are free to explore without
constraint,

Lack of strength won't be your
complaint.

Go to where you have not gone before.

Dare to proceed through the open door.

The realm inside will open to you.

Your future awaits...go through, go through.

Chapter 6

THE SEED

The shared laughter of making popcorn over the fireplace has now settled into a time of relaxation in the glow of the fire. It seems to be a perfect time to venture another question.

"Would You like me to stay in just one area of the hidden place, Lord?"

"I want you to live here," He replies with fervency. "It was never My intention that you come to visit and then slip back out into the frenzy of the world."

He shakes His head. "You will deplete your energy that way. In this secret place you can be at rest because you are in life-union with Me (Heb. 13:21). We're one. As My Spirit unveils the riches and favor that now reside in you, My supernatural strength will flood you with both My might and explosive power" (Eph. 3:16).

He leans forward as if to emphasize a point. "The greater the unveiling you recognize within yourself, the greater your strength. I am your source of strength and your fountain of living water" (Jer. 2:13 KJV).

He sits back with eyes half closed, as though aware of something that I don't know. "The world you see is but a picture of a truer reality. This natural realm is but a shadow of the spiritual. In truth, you are a spirit being who has a soul and lives in a body. Your experiences in this life are but a training ground for your soul."

I stare at Him. This is all news to me.

"Your mind, will and emotions are all part of your soul and were meant to radiate Me. You live in this world but have always been destined to find your way home to where your existence began, in Me. My written word is a mirror, always reflecting who you were meant to be" (Mirror Study Bible, pp. 21, 23).

I give the cobwebs in my head a shake, trying to clear my mind.

"Your five physical senses enable you to gather information from the natural realm. The same five senses of your spirit man act in a similar way in the unseen domain where you live in Me (John 3:13 footnote). For example, as you develop these senses, you will at times discern when spiritual beings are near you. You may smell My scent or that of angels. Many see these angels, even cherubs flying with joy around the top of a room. Some feel the touch of My hand on their shoulders. You'll gradually grow to hear and recognize My voice speaking to you. When I enter your room, your sense of touch may react to My manifest presence. Just as in the natural you can taste the flavor of your favorite food and know that it is good, you can read the Word to taste the flavor of My character and see that I am good" (Ps.34:8 RSV).

He continues. "Without fear, live your life but just remain in Me, the Anointed One. When you stay in My shadow, the enemy of your soul is not able to find or harm you" (Ps. 91). I created every place so wherever you go, I am there. But know that as you quiet yourself in your spirit, there will be trips we take together where no one else will ever come. I draw you to Myself and pour out My love in such a way as it is poured out for no one else."

The light of the fireplace has now become a warm glow. Smoldering embers fill the room with the scent of cedar, and I embrace the closeness of the moment. Kneeling in front of me, He pulls from His pocket a small, ivory rose tinted box in the shape of a seashell. It is highlighted with intricate gold designs. He opens it for me to see what is within. To my surprise, it is not jewelry but a tiny, yellow mustard seed. I look up into His eyes to see there a blending of love and anticipation. Waiting for Him to speak, I know not what to expect.

"With your permission, I will plant this seed of faith in your heart. Every time you exercise that faith, My life within you will grow deeper and more powerful. You will end up rooted in Me and overflowing with the knowledge of how much I love you" (Eph. 3:17-19).

My wide-eyed reaction is to think aloud.
"I'm not worthy of such a gift of trust, Lord. How
can this be? I don't understand, but I won't refuse."
I nod my consent.

With loving care, He positions the seed
inside a lower chamber of my heart. A small prick
is all I feel. I'm aware of its location, but it is not at
all uncomfortable. In an unprecedented way, it
gives me a sense of security. It is a reassuring
reminder of my growing relationship with Him. I
sense my heart reacting to the Master's spark with a
burst of fiery love beginning to spread throughout
my being.

Every time I connect with Him my life
seems to do a fruit-basket-upset. It makes me
wonder what more is awaiting me in this incredible
place of encounters.

Chapter 6

THE WORD/THE MIRROR

Look in the mirror and you will
see

I in you and you in Me.

You're no longer a part of the
dark

But a light in the night.

Together, we shine so white that

Evil must take flight.

Invite others into the Light

Then they too may shine bright.

II Cor. 3:18

Chapter 7

TAKE HEART

The battle will be fierce but you
will overcome.

Hold My hand securely and
together we will run.

The enemy is deceitful...his
weapons, oh, so lethal.

But he'll no longer conquer; his
plans will go down under.

The victory is assured; do not lose
heart, dear soul;

Though vision is obscured, we
will win the goal.

Chapter 7

THE STRONGHOLD

"I can't do this. I don't know how. I don't understand." I slam the mouse down on the desk and burst into sobs. After the wonder of last evening, this has been a long morning of aggravation on the computer. True, my brain is mired in technological mud, but this anger takes me by surprise.

Soft footsteps behind me announce that I'm no longer alone in the dimly lit office next to my bedroom.The Shepherd steadies my rolling desk chair as I turn to stand before Him, my face looking down.

"What are you afraid of?" His calm voice soothes the edges of my irritation.

"I'm not afraid. I'm just so frustrated."

"But fear is buried beneath the frustration. What is it that you fear?"

Tears continue trickling down my cheeks while I think about His question. "I guess I'm afraid I'll never be able to master all these computer problems."

"Do you remember the first time as a little girl when you were frightened?" He asks.

"Yes." My voice quavers a bit. "I stepped into a drop off at Lake Hiddenwood. I went under three times before my feet could again touch solid ground. I feared I would drown. I never told my parents about it. I was too scared."

Taking my hands in His, He speaks. "I know. I was there with you. I saved your life. The enemy wanted to take you out. The fear of drowning is the root of all your other fears. An unresolved emotion can remain stored in your brain and cellular memories. It can become a wall that blocks you out of the safety of My presence. You don't want that. Are you willing to let Me bring it to the surface and heal it?"

I jump at the chance. "I want fear out of my life. Let's take care of this." I bow my head. "Forgive me, Christ Jesus. Help me relax my will and open my heart's door. I see You, standing in Your river of forgiveness, waiting to wash to and through my buried fear. Please, do that and bring Your peace."

I wait in His presence until I feel the gentle waves of His love. It makes me feel so clean (Ps. 51:7). It's soon followed by His precious peace that is beyond all human understanding (Phil 4:7). A wide yawn escapes from deep within, announcing my freedom.

He continues. "Did you make any decisions after what happened to you at the lake?"

"Yes! Don't ever go in deep water again. Protect yourself." My quick, forceful reply catches me off guard. "Oh, Lord." My mouth drops. "I was way in over my head this morning with the computer glitch. That's what triggered fear in me."

"Yes, it's all connected. Unknowingly, when you were at the lake, your natural response was for your mind, will and emotions to work together, finding a quick fix to what made you afraid. But that solution was shaped by the enemy (John 8:44), not by Me. It only magnified your fear over the years and left your heart's door open to other fears. The decision of your will intertwined itself with the trauma. That is what made it so strong. It grew to be an indestructible fortress in your mind—a stronghold (II Cor. 10:4 RSV).

"Something else you tend to do when you're hurt or afraid is to put a Teflon-like covering over your heart and body. You think you're protecting yourself from harm, but you're only insulating yourself from My love and the love of others. I keep on loving you, but your protective suit prevents it from soaking in.

"Often the biggest obstacle is to forgive yourself, especially when you know you've made a decision you regret. Would you be willing to delete that unforgiveness" (Col. 2:14)?

Yes, I forgive myself, totally. I see myself pulling up, out of the lake of unforgiveness, the little girl version of me. I love and affirm her and then give her over into the arms of Jesus. I am much relieved when that 'window' of my life also closes in peace. I no longer need to punish myself. I can just accept and love who I am (Matt. 22:37-39).

"Next," He says, "Was there a lie of the enemy associated with that decision of yours?"

I sense my mind functioning in high-speed internet mode.

"Yes. If I go in deep water, I'll drown."

Lifting my head to look in His eyes, He continues. "You're right. It is a lie. In My Name, reject and renounce it."

My words tumble out. "In the mighty Name of Jesus, I renounce and reject that lie."

"Now, speak out the truth you hear in your heart. What is it?"

I listen and then look up at Him with a wide smile.

"It was a one-time thing. Just because it happened once, doesn't mean it will happen again. I know how to swim. I don't have to be afraid."

"Okay. Declare it to the enemy."

"I can do that, Lord?"

"Yes, I've given you that authority" (Matt. 28:18).

With a confident voice I proclaim that truth.

I hope I am finished with the process, but there's more. "You've recognized and eliminated the lie. Now, take a deep breath. Blow down the remaining empty structure of fear built up in your mind over time" (Josh.5:16).

"Lord, that seems impossible for me to do. It looks so big."

"See it through My eyes," He replies. "Remember, a lie has no substance. It's a house of cards. Because you are forgiven, you carry My power. As you release one deep breath of My Spirit, it will topple (II Cor. 10:3-4). Try it."

I doubt this is going to work, but I take a big breath and blow with all my might. To my amazement, I see the imaginary fortress crumble. With mouth agape and eyes wide, I stare up at Him. He laughs as I begin to comprehend the reality of what has just happened. I'm delighted. I'm free. I'm a victor instead of a victim (Rom. 8:37). Joy bubbles up in me. This was easy. Just for fun, I take another breath to blow away the debris.

"Well done, little one. There will be other strongholds to topple. But the first one lies demolished. Others will follow suit at the proper time. An enemy fortress is always a cheap imitation. I am your true 'castle on a cliff, your forever firm fortress'" (Ps. 18:1-2).

He steps behind me to position Himself as my protector. "Always remember, I've got your back, no matter what comes against you. My glory is your rear guard" (Is. 58:8 RSV). Resting His chin

on the top of my head, He gives me a warm,
brotherly hug.

"It's been so many years since I've let
anyone close enough to touch my heart. You came
to help when no one else did. You, the Great
Forgiver, took away my trauma, hurt and pain. You
set me free" (John 8:36).

After a bit, He moves in front of me. "I'm
not only behind you, but I also go before you to
prepare the way (Deut.1:30 RSV). I will never leave
you or forsake you" (Deut. 31:6 RSV).

Looking down at the computer, He asks,
"How do you feel about this little issue now?"

I turn to glance at it, and reply with a smile,
"It's okay. I'm not afraid anymore. We'll handle it
together" (Col 3:14 RSV).

Chapter 7

SUNSHINE

May the Lord of sunshine light
your way.

May skies no longer be dark and
gray.

He goes before you to make a
way.

Walk through the door and see
His way.

Chapter 8

THE JOY OF LOVE

I'm so in love with You, my King

I'm bursting at the seams...

My heart, rejoicing, in life that
springs anew.

Never can I get enough of You.

Come, dance with me.

Come, sing with me.

Let our hearts become as one

As we romp together in the sun!

Chapter 8

THE VERANDA OF LOVE

Each new day brings more of a sharpened awareness of the King's quiet presence beside me. As I become acclimated to my new position in Him, I notice His clothing carries just the hint of aromatic incense (Ps 45:8).

Right now though, my growling stomach is putting me on notice that it is breakfast time. Hurrying out the door and toward the kitchen, I run into the Master along the way. Hunger pangs all but disappear in the excitement of the moment. I blurt out, "Lord, will You Yourself go with me and show me more of this dwelling place?"

He seems pleased I've asked, but pauses a while, looking down at me, as if considering what to do. A look I've not seen before crosses His face. All at once, He grabs my hand. With the excitement of two youngsters on an adventure, we move out in a direction I've not been before.

We soon pass through glass French doors, swinging open to a spacious, white veranda alive with the freshness of an early morning sunrise. Standing beside one another, admiring the brilliant colors of dawn, He drapes His arm over my shoulder. Between us there is only a sense of total openness. I feel as though I could pour out all my life's secrets and still be loved.

The fiery hues of daybreak shimmer around us. They begin to quicken within me the embers of a burning love existing long before creation (Eph. 1:4a). I look inward and realize that even now His unseen Spirit is searching for open pathways. He seems intent on restoring that original love back into my fractured heart.

His healing balm continues to soothe my wounds until His work is complete and peace again reigns (Col. 3:15). Looking up at Him, I see nothing but a reflection of the love in His heart. With the inner roadblocks removed, I am again free to turn my attention outward.

The panorama of an untouched garden landscape spreads out from the veranda. Its beauty lies before my wondering gaze. I hum the words of a song learned as a little girl. "He walks with me and He talks with me…and the joy we share as we tarry there, none other has ever known." I realize this is the case now. We will be the only ones to ever enjoy this unique garden of existence within the hidden place.

He smiles as if in agreement. "With eagerness, Adam and Eve got to explore together the unblemished Garden of Eden. Now every person who is a new creation can do the same (II Cor. 5:17 RSV). Each gets to have his own private adventures in Me."

As undiluted peace closes in on us, He gathers me close to Himself with a gentleness I've not before experienced. My expectant heart waits for Him to speak. When He does, it is in low tones near my ear. His voice carries a passion echoing from ages long gone.

"I have waited for this moment from eternity past (John 1:2 footnote)…you are now Mine, and I am yours."

His words settle within me. My spirit responds, melting like wax in warm surrender. All else fades from my vision as my inner being is overcome by a love that gives, asking nothing in return.

After an undetermined passage of time, consciousness again begins to take form through colored clouds of mist. A sunflower comes into focus with a young girl standing in front of it. With careful hesitancy, she is pulling petals off the ripened head of the flower. "He loves me; he loves me not. He loves me; he loves me not."

But in the stillness of my heart, with tears streaming down my face, I cry out in joy, "He loves me; He loves me; He loves me."

No doubt remains. The truth is now settled in my heart. I have been forever loved, and nothing can ever separate me from that love (Rom. 8:38-39).

Chapter 8

CONSUMMATION

Consummation—

Oh, what is here contained in one word...

The end of all things, the beginning of all things.

Earth cannot comprehend it,

Heaven cannot contain it,

Time has preceded it,

Centuries have spanned it.

It burns in the heart,

It leaps to the spirit,

It pursues eternity.

Chapter 9

MY EVERYTHING

Lord, make me hungry...for the
savor of You.

Let my soul be athirst...for the
living You.

Let my heart be aflame...with the
fire of You.

Let my eyes reflect...my delight
in You.

Let my hands reach out...for the
closeness of You.

You are my everything.

You are my King.

"Thou whom my soul loveth."

Song of Sg. 1:7b

Chapter 9

THE LIBRARY

My bare feet sink into the softness of the luxurious burgundy carpet. The afternoon is warm and humid as the Master walks beside me in a slow, relaxed manner. The only sound punctuating the silence of the wide corridor is our light conversation and easy laughter. Over the past few days, I've become aware of a growing solidness of faith that was not there before. I'm excited to be able to tell Him about this.

I see open double doors ahead of us. To my delight, He leads me through them and into a sunlit library. A light breeze drifting through the lace curtained window brings with it the scent of fresh spring rain. There is about the room an impression of simplicity and peace.

To our right stands a gilded, antique reading table. On top is a fresh loaf of baked bread, homemade butter and pomegranate preserves (Song of Sg. 7:12). Two half-filled glasses of red wine complete the setting.

Since I've always taken great delight in books, I am eager to begin exploring. On the mahogany shelves I notice countless leather-bound volumes of Scripture in all languages. Some are ancient with embossed covers; others look like they've just been checked out of a hometown library. Glancing through various other books, however, I see many of those pages blank. I stand there, puzzled.

He beckons for me to join Him at the table while we visit. I find myself savoring every bite of the bread. It tastes as delicious as it smells. It reminds me of the honey wheat bread my mother would bake every Saturday morning on the farm.

He begins sharing with me. As He does, I discover His words convey the insight of the one and only Teacher (Is. 30:19-21).

"You see, the hidden place is one of trust. There is no room here for the natural mind with its speculations and wrong thinking (II Cor. 10:3-4 RSV). Remember, I am the Truth. Without Me you can do nothing (John 15:5b RSV). Here in My library, the words and pages written without My breath of life upon them are of no eternal value. Thus, some pages are blank."

I cannot help but cling to His every word while my heart burns within me (Luke 24:32).

"With great expertise, the natural mind can gather information to form conclusions, but trust has to do with relationship. We enter through trust into the kingdom. This entire realm operates in love, joy and peace. There is a flow to it. Self-effort falls flat because it has no life. It's like stale bread. It attracts no one. But people are drawn to Me, the fresh bread, for their nourishment, energy and power every day. They will search Me out for they've learned only in Me are hidden all the treasures of wisdom and knowledge" (Col. 2:3).

He leans forward and continues, "You will always feel at home in this room. You will also grow to find this a place of deep intimacy with Me. Noise, distractions and pain are a part of your natural environment. There you often experience sensory overload. It can seem as though you are living in the Tower of Babel (Gen. 11:1-9). Here you will discover a hidden oasis, receiving both gladness and breakthrough" (Ps. 32:7).

He speaks with more deliberation now. "You have immediate access to Me here, surrounded by My Word, the bread and wine. My identity and purpose have always been intertwined with these tangible elements. They will always be here for you."

As He smiles and gestures for me to partake of more of the healing bread, He comments, "You know, don't you, that I am the ultimate 'staff of life' and the new wine? I am offering to you Myself— everything you will ever need" (Eph. 1:22a).

Worship and praise fill my heart as my eyes lock on to His. Therein we see the depths of ignited love reflected in one another. Tender, grateful tears begin overflowing their banks. They stream down my cheeks as I take again of the bread and lift my glass to His.

His offer is accepted.

Chapter 9

TOUCH ME

Touch Me in all the details of
your life.

Reach out to Me...

with a glance, a thought,

a smile or cry,

a longing, a yielding,

with a grasping of My hand,

a leaning in My direction,

with an inhaling of My scent or

a tasting of My bread and wine.

Ps. 18:1 (Footnote)

Chapter 10

THE PATH OF LIFE

There is a path that lies stretched
before you.

It is the path of life.

See it not?

It is there...

At times, obscured by the
deceiver,

But, still...beckoning you further

With a glimpse of its fiery
diamonds reflecting the Son.

Fear not, My little one.

I go before you to light the way.

I guide you into each new day.

Psalm 16:11

Exodus 15:13 RSV

Chapter 10

THE BLESSING

Valentine's Day—the day of love. My first one in the hidden place. The banqueting table in the grand dining room is still laden to over-flowing with abundance. The scents of red wine vinegar over roasted salmon and the cinnamon and nutmeg baked rice still mingle in the air with freshly cut oranges and lemons. It's been a delightful meal with the King of Hearts Who has given me His constant attention throughout our time together. In the flickering candlelight our eyes meet often, ever watching for the reaction of the other; and yet, comfortable as though we've known each other forever. There's an easy exchange of conversation balanced with a rich silence, engaging hearts only.

The experience is a touching of love on a day of love.

It has been a partaking not only of savory food but also of the richness of Him–the Bread of Life and the Living Water (Ps. 36:7-9). I feel as though I have been marinated both in His Word and Himself to the point of saturation. However, as He rises from the padded velour dining room chair and comes to rest His hands on my head (Ps.139:5), I realize there is yet more to come.

The blessing.

In the sweetness of the moment, He begins.

"I will open your eyes and you will hear a word behind you saying this is the way, walk in it, when you turn to the right or when you turn to the left (Is. 30:21 RSV). I will encompass you with My very Self. My presence will go before you, and I will give you peace (Ex. 33:14 RSV). Walk in it. I will direct your every step" (Prov. 3:5-8).

With each word He speaks, there is a distillation of peace settling into the pores of my spirit.

"Learn of Me for I am humble and lowly, and you will find rest for your soul. My yoke is easy, and My burden is light (Matt. 11:28-30). My face will continuously shine on You and give you peace (Num. 6:24-26 RSV). I will light the way before you. Know that in Me there is no shame. In the world there is shame, but in Me is only acceptance and love (Ps. 34:5).

"I care for you. I help you stand. I teach you how to walk before Me in the land of the living; and afterwards, I will receive you into glory (Ps.116: 8-10 RSV). Up until now, you have walked with Me on the surface of the landscape of life. Now I will take you into a deeper walk with Me where you will plow virgin soil in the spirit realm, and your fruit will endure (John 15:16). It will not be stolen by the enemy (John 10:10). I will take you where none has gone before, a new way. I will chart for you a new course, and you will lean into Me heavily (Song of Sg. 8:5). It will be only My strength infusing you and bringing forth the fruit."

I sit up even straighter in my mahogany chair, straining to not miss or forget one of His words.

"Learn of Me, I say again, for I am humble and lowly of heart. Watch how I will help you finish tasks with a minimum of effort and little loss of energy. My way is easy. Your boat of life at times will be loaded with cargo. None of it is to be lost, so sail only in the current of peace within you (Col. 3:15). Then you and your boat will safely reach your destination in Me" (John 6:16-21).

His hands continue to rest on me while His words find their home within me. I am awed by the import of this blessing. I sense it will be the challenge of a lifetime to walk it out. But for now, on this day of love, my vital energies have been replenished, my affections renewed, and my desires rekindled. It is enough.

Chapter 10

THE BOAT

Swept out to sea in a boat of love,
Driven by the wind of God above.
Adventure high my soul does feel.
This is life—this is real.

He sees the path and knows the way.
I yield to Him my will and say,
"At Your feet my life I lay,
Take it, bless it, now I pray."

Chapter 11

THE PROCESS

Shine Your light in me,
Show me all that I can be.

Shine Your light in me,
Show me Your path for me.

Light Your path in me,
So Your treasure I can see.

Light Your treasure in me,
So Your fruit others can see.

Light Your fruit in me,
So others Your love can see.

Light Your love in me,
So others Your peace can see.

Light Your peace in me,
So others Your Son can see.

Chapter 11

THE PROCESS

I wake the next morning bright and eager for the start of this new day. My heart, filled with the wonder of last evening, aches for more of Him. Wrapping my arms around my pillow, as though holding Him near, I whisper.

"I long to be one with You, Lord, to really know You (II Cor. 4:6). Not just on and off, here and there, bit by bit. I no longer want to be separate from You. I want to be in Your presence all the time."

I sound like a love-sick schoolgirl, but I don't care. I wash up, throwing on the nearest clean clothes–my bright red sweater with the three pink valentines on the front and my fancy pocketed blue jeans. My feet have a mind of their own as they skip down the stairs and into the breakfast area. My heart leaps to find the King already seated at the oak table waiting for me. The scent of warm ham and cheese croissants beckons me, along with fragrant coffee, cantaloupe slices and luscious red grapes.

We bow our heads in thanks to Father for the food we get to eat, and then words come tumbling out of my mouth.

"Last evening was amazing in every way, and the meal was sumptuous. I've been reliving it throughout the night. I have a question though, my Lord. Why do people come to Your banqueting table and just take a little taste of You and leave?"

"Just like babies," He answers between bites, "they can get air bubbles of the enemy in their tummies, and a little taste is all they have room for."

"Air bubbles of the enemy? I don't understand."

"They are his bait—unforgiveness, anger, envy, bitterness—empty lies that trick us. We take them in without realizing.

"How does one get them out then, to make room for more of You?"

"The longer you remain soaking in the light of My love, and the longer you linger in My presence," He smiles, "the more darkness of the deceiver is revealed (Lk. 8:16-18). Let's say you find an air bubble of doubt. Here's what you do. In repentance, breathe in My Spirit. The bubble of doubt will rise to the surface. It might even be expelled in the form of a yawn. In this way you will be making room for the milk of My Word."

My croissant is only half-eaten, but I am hungrier for His words than for the food on my plate. His words are living bread, filled with life.

"How are the nutrients of Your Word absorbed in us, Lord? What is the process?"

"Let's use one verse as an example of what happens. 'Behold, God is my salvation; I will trust, and will not be afraid; for the LORD GOD is my strength and my song, and He has become my salvation.' (Is.12:2 RSV). First it enters your mind. There your brain explores the facts, like finding the meaning to the word salvation and its synonyms. Next, your will enters the picture. It must decide if it will trust or be afraid. Just to give you a heads up, you will find trusting a whole lot easier than wasting your precious energy fighting fear. Trusting is operating in the ease of the Spirit.

"I have made you mysteriously complex" (Ps.139:14). As you continue, there will be a deeper progression into truth. You will see Me as I really am (Col. 3:4). You will be more aware of Me. Godly emotions will be activated. You will feel joy rising. My joy is always there, but now it will surface, being released in laughter and song. The last step is my truth becoming real within you. Not only has your mind understood and received My Word, but now your heart will also grab hold and take it in as its very own possession.

"Awareness of the completion of that final stage is when you sense down in your gut that you know that you know that you know I am your salvation. It is now personal and real; it is rooted in the fertile soil of your spirit being. It is reality within you; it cannot slip away or be stolen by the enemy of your soul."

He reaches for the written word laying on the table. I notice He handles The Book with such ease and grace, as though it were a part of Himself (John 1:1). Opening it to the Isaiah passage, He welcomes me to read it back to Him. He enjoys hearing what He has written, and it helps me inscribe it in my memory. As I read, I sense His words sinking deep within me as though filling a vacancy I hadn't realized was there.

A change in the atmosphere breaks my attention and causes me to return my gaze to Him. There is a tangible supernatural power emanating from Him (Lk. 6:19). I am irresistibly drawn to the life spilling out of His words and countenance. I can't get enough of Him. He reads me like an open book and reassures me with His reply. "How filled you become when you are consumed with hunger and desire, for you will be completely satisfied" (Lk. 6:21). My heart is soothed with His answer and presence across the table. This is not the end but only the beginning.

Chapter 11

THE YEARNING

Tears watering my ears
As side to side my head turns...
My heart yearns,
Yearns
For more of You...
More of You
Inside of me—
Fill me,
Love me,
Hold me.

Chapter 12

I KNOW

The hurt is so real

The pain so deep.

The scars so real

The emptiness so deep.

"I know," says the Master.

"My hurt was so real

My pain so deep.

My scars so real

My emptiness so deep.

But...if you will surrender to Me

your hurt,

pain,

your scars and

loss,

I will apply My salve of love

to heal the hurt,

soothe the pain,

transform the scars and

fill the void."

I know you; I love you. You are
Mine.

Is. 43:1

THE YIELDING

He comes looking for me (Matt.18:11-14). He finds me beyond the open door of the pearly white bathroom where I have hidden myself in shame. The carnage of the broken pieces of my heart are lying all over the floor.

His unexpected entrance brings a glimmer of light, but I still sit huddled with dejection in the far corner. My fuzzy, brown blanket is draped over my shoulders for comfort amid my tears. I feel so alone, but hope is a given when the King of Love enters the room.

At the sight of His pierced feet before me, I sob, "I'm so sorry, my Lord. I'm so, so sorry."

In my hands I clutch a silver, glittering idol. I try to hide it from His view; but, of course, He sees all. Nothing is hidden from Him (Ps. 139:7-10).

Christ, the Forgiver, pauses for a time and then, with a gentle but firm grip, helps me to my feet. I cannot lift my eyes to His. The shameful darkness within prevents me from meeting His gaze.

"I'm so confused. I don't know what to do. I have sinned against You. I've placed this idol on the throne of my heart instead of exalting only You. I'm no longer worthy to be called Your daughter." Great tears roll down my cheeks. "Forgive me, Lord. Help me" (Luke 15:19).

In an instant, with that cry for help, His hands open to receive the small silver idol. Yet, even then, my will does not yield what it has so long treasured. Its grip on me is too great. I lack the power to surrender it.

Calling out again, I plead, "Have Your way in me, to do what pleases You (Phil. 2:13). Help!"

As tears continue their free flow, I lift my eyes to His in utter desperation. At once, all fullness of compassion flows from Him, flooding me with His grace (Eph. 2:1-4).

Now empowered, my will yields. I quickly place the alluring item into His hands before I can change my mind. It crumbles into ashes at His touch and so does the part of my heart that was stone. In the light of His presence my spirit eyes open, and I see the insignificance of what I had in pride so magnified.

To my amazement, I am aware that even my point of view is now shifting into alignment with His. That is not the only thing undergoing a change. I see the hard, bulldog appearance of my will softening right before my eyes—beginning to take on the more becoming features of the Master's countenance (Eph. 4:23-24).

He speaks, His eyes smiling at me. "When you were born, I inscribed hope upon your soul because hope fulfilled is a tree of life (Prov. 13:12 RSV). You need hope to survive."

Now a river of love begins flowing from His Spirit into my emotional core. As it does, my load of guilt is washed away by His clean waters of forgiveness. The idol is gone, and my sprinkled heart has again become a heart of flesh (Ez. 36:25-26).

With Him I sit and rest for a time on the marble bench. He leans over to ask, "What have you learned from all this, my little one?"

Pausing, I place my hand in His before answering. "I think of all the things, good and beautiful, You've put in my life. They're all a gift from You. I'm in danger though when I prioritize those gifts as being of more value than You. Keep me safe from falling into that trap again."

His arm goes around my shoulder, pulling me closer. The coolness of the seat and the nearness of His presence bring a sharp awareness of the truth. When I put into His hands the puzzle pieces of my life, it will form a beautiful picture with Him at the center. Then, He will be able to trust into my hands His fiery white holiness.

The approval in His eyes says it all. Jubilation jumps up and down inside of me while the harp inside my heart makes music to Him. "My God, I will sing you a brand-new song" (Ps. 144:9).

I rejoice for I know my heart is healed; my will is yielded, and I am His!

Chapter 12

TRANSFORMATION

I saw you in the darkness, bowed
deep and low,

Your eyes downcast, your speech
so very slow.

No light within you shone,

You felt so all alone.

I called you from the darkness,

I softly spoke your name.

"Come to me for peacefulness.

You'll never be the same."

You rise up out of darkness

And My light shines therein.

Your heart is filled with
brightness.

You're washed of every sin.

Now from the other side of
darkness

You call many to the light.

You lead them out of blindness...

Into hope and sight.

Eph. 4:23-24

Chapter 13

ONE TO BEHOLD

*In the darkness of the night, in
the stillness of the soul
There goes One forth...
One to Behold.*

*His eyes burn like fire
And there's a depth to His soul
That only He can know.*

*His eyes light the way into my
night,
And into my soul...
The way only He can know.*

He fills my night and He fills my
soul

And a song goes forth

From the One to Behold.

"Come into My light. Come into
My soul.

Together we'll go forth

The world to uphold."

Chapter 13

THE DOOR

The Shepherd joins me at the outskirts of the hidden place. The overcast sky threatens to break out in a shower at any moment. The scent of freshly turned over soil fills my nostrils as I keep watch over my mother's newly dug grave. It's been over four months since her death; but because of the snow and frozen ground, we've just now been able to bury her body.

He kneels beside me as I weep great tears of grief and loss (John 11:33). Renewed sorrow spills over the reservoir of my heart and takes on a life of its own as it pours over my lips. "My mom is gone. She knew me better than anyone else in the entire world, and now she's not here with me anymore. I miss her so. I'm all alone now."

My mind knows that not all the words tumbling out of my mouth are true, but my heart is swamped with self-pity. I feel as though I don't have the strength to fight anymore (I Tim. 6:12 RSV). I surrender to the heaviness that over-whelms me and fall face down on my hands beside the closed grave. All the while His presence never strays.

After a time, my tears cease, and an awareness of my situation rises to the forefront of my mind. I realize I need to escape this self-imposed prison. I can't stay here like this. I turn my attention back to Him, crying out, "Lord, have mercy on me now. Heal me" (Mark 10:48).

Within my heart I hear His words, "I am the Resurrection, and I am Life Eternal. Anyone who clings to Me in faith, even though he dies, will live forever" (John 11:25).

His next words are a calm command. "Stand up."

I open my red swollen eyes to look around. He's no longer beside me but positioned at the head of the grave. His stance is that of a victor; yet, at the same time, the center of Him fades into a vague impression of a door (John 10:9 RSV).

I stand and intuitively know I am to approach Him. With a hope I barely dare to acknowledge, I step up close.

Is there more to life than this? I wonder.

He reaches out both arms to draw me to Himself. To my great surprise, however, I am not pulled to Him, but through Him, as though He has no material body at all. I now find myself in the ethereal atmosphere of heaven.

To my utter amazement all grief, sorrow, pain and pity vanish; it's all been left on the other side. I am instantly healed, restored, delivered and rescued (Mark 10:52 footnote). Nothing of the old remains. I am transformed in the sparkling realities of the kingdom (Col. 3:2). My entire being is awash with His righteousness, joy and peace (Rom. 14:17-18).

"I can see now, Lord, through Your eyes. I can see how things really are (Eph. 1:18; Rev. 3:18b-19). This is what my mother is experiencing. I remember her telling me how she and her friend had invited You into their hearts as little girls on the steps of their small country church. You, Jesus, have lived in her heart most of her ninety-eight years on this earth, and now she is living in Your heart. How fitting.

He holds out His hand for me to step back again into the reality of this natural realm. With tiny, silent droplets of spring rain settling over us, I remain beside the grave and ponder this beautiful portrait of oneness.

"I see, Good Shepherd, as we open our hearts' doors to Your knocking (Rev. 3:20), so will You open Your heart to our knocking because You know us (Luke 13:22-30). Thank you, my King, for being the entrance, the gate, to not only a life in heaven but also to the start of that life right here and now. I can always be secure and growing in You, the living hidden place."

With a sigh of relief, I relax. "The hidden place is wherever You are; and I can enter in anytime, anywhere."

A beautiful stillness settles over us as the sun begins shining through the clouds. Together we

turn and walk away from the shadow of death into
the radiance of life, hope and dreams yet to come.

"Swing wide, you gates of righteousness, and let me
pass through,

and I will enter into Your presence to worship only
you!

I have found the gateway to God,

The pathway to His presence for all His lovers."

Psalm 118:19-20

Chapter 13

PEACE

Peace...

It is a seed, you know.

It must be cultivated to grow.

It must be cared for and nursed along

While it is tender and not yet strong.

It must become familiar within you

To become tried, firm and true.

Be sure to treasure it within your heart

So that from it, you will not depart.

Chapter 14

THE FIELD

All was ready...

the rocks were cleared from the
field of love.

Then...

with slow approach,
all pervading, all encompassing,

there came...
a heavy Presence,
with such tenderness and love,

a Presence...

that settled down
from above.

Oh...
such tenderness
such love!

Chapter 14

THE FIELDS OF GRACE

The bright afternoon sun bathes me in warmth as I lounge in the quiet of the veranda garden. This soaking is interrupted though by a sudden shiver running up and down my spine. Just when I detect the sweet scent of henna blossoms (Song of Sg. 1:14), His familiar hand grabs mine.

With joyous expectation the King calls out, "Let's go," and off we swoop out of the garden and over the slopes below.

We are moving at a breathtaking pace so there is little time to absorb the scope of what I am seeing. It's a panorama of beckoning trails leading off in all directions. Below me is a multi-colored tapestry of blue, pink, yellow and purple blossoms gracing the fields (I Peter 4:10). It is a wonder to behold.

A wooden Dutch windmill stands as a focal point at the top of a hill. Grazing deer dot the landscape. Young rabbits at play dart in and out of red mulberry bushes. Whimsical groupings of tulips are interwoven in the most delightful, free-spirited manner. Rivulets wend their way down the lush, green hillsides, watering the plants and creating small ponds here and there. My heart leaps with pleasure and joy at the sight of it all (I Cor. 1:3 footnote).

Never in my wildest dreams have I imagined such a place of natural beauty and plenty. Random clusters of plants and trees are intermingled in the most surprising ways. I could sit in one spot all day long to just absorb the magnificence of it all.

Heady with the stimulation of both sight and smell, I realize that as I've moved with Him, I have been caught up into a live streaming of the fields of grace (II Peter 1:2). I've just seen a living representation of undeserved, overflowing goodness from the hand of the Lord. I would be content to stay here forever.

He has other plans. As we near the bottom of the slopes, we settle down in the midst of a spacious grove of willows, interspersed with occasional olive and elm trees.

Adventure fills His voice. "Come dance with Me in this field of grace."

In a twinkling He lifts me high in the air and twirls me round and round—my layered, pink chiffon dress billowing in the breeze, and my head whirling in joy. Slipping back again into His strong arms, we dance until we can dance no more (Song of Sg. 8:14).

At the edge of the clearing, we fall exhausted onto the thick, velvety grass where countless flowers release their delicate wisps of perfume. We lie gasping for breath and laughing with the pure joy of life. Every peel of laughter is funnier than the last.

Exhausted, my body finally gives in to rest. In due course, a supernatural strength infuses my core (Is. 41:10), spreading its restoration to every muscle and cell of my body (Heb. 4:12). For a long time, I soak in His peace (Ps. 4:8 RSV). All the while rays of sunlight shine upon us through gilt-edged clouds radiating His glory.

I immerse myself in the quiet perception of His presence near me. My spirit, however, again feels drawn, rising to meet His. The only awareness remaining within is of the fiery flame that is Him (I Peter 1:8).

"But the one who joins himself to the Lord is mingled into one spirit with him."

(I Cor. 6:17)

Chapter 14

JOY

To Play—

Free

Frisky

Fun

To Dance—

Glide

Swirl

Twirl

To Live—

Be

Love

Give

Chapter 15

THE SEARCH

"Spring up, O Well" of Living
Water...

let Your presence arise within.

Enfold.

Engulf.

Envelop.

Let Your glory wash over me.

Liquify my spirit,

merging it with Yours,

immersing me in the depths of
the hidden life

while searching for the Pearl of
great price...

finding it hidden deep within—

the treasure of Him.

Numbers 21:17 RSV

Chapter 15

THE WELL

Beads of perspiration glisten on my hot forehead in the bright afternoon sunshine. However, curiosity urges me forward. A grass-covered pathway in a neglected area of the garden intrigues me. Now, pushing aside a bit of underbrush, I spot an old stone well in this unfrequented nook. Lush green moss outlines each worn stone. Dangling from the winch is a long, slender rope, frayed with age. A hand-carved cedar cup is knotted to the end of it, just waiting to be noticed. Somehow, it looks familiar.

I try my hand at drawing water, but only end up with my mouth more parched.

The Lord strolls up behind me. "May I tell you how best to do it?"

I nod in grateful eagerness.

"You will want to start first with the cup, emptying it of dust and debris that may have accumulated there. Hold it close to yourself. It is a representation of you. After learning to cherish the 'you' within, your heart will be primed to receive this water of life. Next, expect the emptiness inside to be filled. See with the eyes of your spirit the sparkling living water. Then step up to the well again, not doubting, but believing, that the water here is not just for others, but for you too.

"Would you like some?"

"Oh yes," I say. "Please help me."

This time, with Him at my side, I am bursting with faith as I begin the learning process.

In no time at all, He has reknotted the cup handle to the rope, making it more secure. With careful attention, He begins to let it drop.

He explains to me the surface water will fill my cup with the water of salvation. "Many drink here with joy and are fully satisfied (Is. 12:3). It also brings Me the greatest satisfaction, for that is the reason I gave My life. But the longer and more expectantly we wait for the cup to go lower, the deeper and richer will be the revelation and insight we draw up" (Ps. 36:9).

He continues, "There are those, however, whose hearts' desires begin to increase until they want to draw from the wellspring itself. They would let out the rope, not only to the bottom of the well, but take it a step further. They would allow it to be carried in the current of My Spirit to the very origin of the spring of life (Rev. 22:1).

"There, at the source, is only stillness and peace. There are no distractions or contaminations of any kind. That is where the truest, purest water is found, resulting in complete union with the One Who Is."

Bringing the cup to the surface, He turns, offering it to me (John 4:10). It is overflowing with the crystal-clear water of life (Rev. 22:1).

Raising the cup to my lips, my eyes also lift to His. In amazement, I see His clear eyes have now taken on an almost fluid appearance, reflecting within Himself the bottomless living water (John 7:37-38).

"Drink of Me." The invitation seems to come in the form of waves echoing down the corridor of time. It resounds in the chambers of my heart with an unexpected familiarity—like I've heard it before, but only in the background of my consciousness. Now that it is front and center, I realize it's been an offer I've been longing to accept.

With an eagerness surprising even me, I take my first swallow of the precious liquid. To my delight, the inner thirst is quenched in an instant. At the same time, I am overcome with an intense yearning for more of Him. I fall to my knees, pouring out my heart as a living drink offering (Num. 28:7). In so doing, I allow myself to sink even deeper into the waters of the living God where I become one with Him.

Chapter 15

ENGULFED IN THE DEEP

"Come with Me."

We leap into the well so deep.

*The waters swirl above, but in
the deep*

there is a pull and a sweep...

deeper and

deeper,

further and

further we are carried along.

There is no fear.

Spirit to spirit we are carried...

*swept to the source where time
began its course.*

*There remains only the stillness
of the deep,*

the peace of the deep,

the closeness of the deep.

There, the two become one...

in purpose,

in rest,

in being.

Chapter 16

ENFOLDING

Enfold me today in Your love
Descending straight from above,
Wrapping me near in Your
peace,
Lending my life a new lease.

For this is the season to shine
In intimacy with the Divine,
Releasing His love on the earth,
Sparking His kingdom's new
birth.

Stroll easily with Him through
this day.

Surrender—let Him have His say.

His delight, having you at His
side

His yearning, to be near His new
bride.

Chapter 16

THE SURRENDER

What a goldmine of learning I have stumbled upon.

As a teacher by trade, I thrive in this atmosphere sparkling with fresh insights. I find in the hidden place "spiritual realities are only discovered" in one way— "by the illumination of His Spirit" (I Cor. 2:12-14). This is new for me.

I also find that the Lord of all Wisdom seems to wait in anticipation of my inquisitiveness. His answers are open and honest. Today I come prepared, not so much with a question, but a longing for reassurance. Settling down on the couch next to Him, I bask again in the soothing light of His presence. It not only warms me, but it also heals me. As I soak in that soft radiance, I venture into the subject I have been pondering.

"Would You please tell me more about Your love for me?"

"But of course I will," is His quick, earnest reply.

"In answer, I take you back to the cross. It was the scene of My most formidable trial and My supreme victory. Every drop of blood was for you,

My Beloved. The agony was great, but the longing for My Bride was even greater."

His words open to me the very door of His heart.

"I had you on My mind—My love for you and My future joy in you. I could already see Myself rejoicing over you with singing and dancing (Zeph. 3:17). I focused on those scenes and on My Father to give me the inner strength to stay on that cross."

The tenderness in His eyes glows as He turns to search my face. "You were the reason I came to earth—to redeem you, to buy you back as My own. My love has now reached again through time and eternity, drawing you into My arms of love to make you one with Me."

My heart fills with the wonder of it all (Ps. 72:118).

"You died for me because You loved me."

The awe of that reality begins invading my heart. The somberness in His eyes and slow, emphatic nod engage my thoughts in a new direction.

"I used to think of surrendering to You in terms of what I would have to give up in some gigantic trial. Now I think of it more in terms of Your filling my empty places with Yourself. Every time I release another portion of my will, I make more room for the treasure of You. I find myself being transformed into the person You always meant me to be."

A sense of excitement grows even as I speak. "There's now a realization of gaining in surrender rather than losing. Instead of it being a negative, it's now a positive. I can look forward to the release of self because I'll be better for it."

"That's how I felt about the sacrifice of the cross. I embraced it in obedience knowing I would be richer for it in the long run" (Heb. 12:2). He smiles. "You see, in surrender we both gained. We gained one another."

With that realization in the forefront of my thoughts, He gathers my heart into His arms. There, in gratitude, I surrender to Love, and Truth becomes reality.

Chapter 16

SURRENDER

My King,

My Love,

My All in All...

I'm Yours.

Do with me according to Your will...

cleanse me in Your blood,

mark me with Your sign,

wrap me in Your arms,

fill me with Yourself,

hold me in Your love.

Proverbs 15:33

Chapter 17

THE FIRE

The fire yet burns…

The embers still glow…

Spring up fresh wind,

Sweep over a love now dim.

Fan into life anew

The hope and faith that I once
knew.

Tend the fire, my Lord King.

Stir my first love until it sings

With joy and laughter from a
heart

That is to You, alone, set apart.

Chapter 17

THE BURNING FIRE

After a light lunch of shrimp salad and warm croissants with honey (Rev. 10:10, footnote), we stroll back to the library. Enjoying one another's company, we take our time. I feel so free and innocent when I am tucked away in His presence (Ps. 34:22).

Again, my attention is drawn to the iridescent sheen of the pearly walls. I ask, "Why do they seem so alive?"

"Everything I created reflects Me and carries My fingerprints. Does not all creation shout of My existence," He asks (Rom. 1:19-21)? "Objects do not have a spirit such as you have, but My attributes are easily perceived through them and displayed by them. Just think of the mighty mountains, thundering waterfalls and flowing rivers. In their unique way, they communicate life."

His tone is confident and loving. "You limit your world by what you perceive through your five senses. When you begin to use the senses of your spirit, your world will expand more than you ever imagined. Do not restrict yourself. Here, in the hidden place, you will learn to better navigate the unseen realm. Lean into Me. Trust Me. I will speak into your ear what you need to know.

"I do not want our time together to be a one-sided relationship," He shares. "I want it to be a give and take as it was with Adam (Rev. 4:16), Eve and Enoch (Gen. 3:8; 5:24 RSV). We walked, talked and interacted on a regular basis. It was a dynamic relationship for us." He smiles at the remembrance. I smile with Him, thinking back to times I sat at my kitchen table sharing with family and friends.

After a pause, my thoughts return to the present, and I feel encouraged to continue the conversation. "Since you are my loving Friend Who is joined to my heart (Prov. 18:24), I feel free to ask about another thing. What happens when You fill me to overflowing? Help me understand, please."

His face brightens as He begins. "Imagine a tea kettle with boiling water on the stove. Hot excess steam is escaping out of the spout. As the droplets enter the atmosphere around the kettle, you no longer see them because they've been absorbed into the environment. After a time though, the air can become so saturated that droplets of water will appear again on a nearby window."

I nod, beginning to follow His line of thinking.

"So it is with My Spirit Who is the fullness of Me. My Spirit cannot be seen; but, just like the wind or the air, He can fill the spiritual atmosphere around you. As you keep the fire of love burning and the heat of its flame increasing, the fullness of Me will begin to fill the empty places within you. Remain in Me and you will also "drip" on the window of the world with the overflow.

"You make everything so understandable, my Lord King." I shake my head at the wonder of it all. "But, then again, You are Wisdom Incarnate, aren't You?" I chuckle to myself.

His expectant expression prompts me to go on to another topic, but a loud noise in the next room turns my attention from Him to the natural world. To my disappointment, I allow this distraction to interrupt our conversation in the heavenly realm (Col. 3:2).

This brief incident teaches me a huge lesson. Be aware of and take captive every thought that would draw me away from His presence and usher me out of the hidden place.

In quick fashion, I ask His forgiveness. In return, He responds with a gentle squeeze of my hand.

I relax back into peace, knowing all is well.

THE FLAMING FIRE

Whence comes the fire?

It comes from the heart of God.

Lightning flashes.

Thunder cracks.

Fire strikes,

ignites,

burns.

Fire carries the Father's flame of love.

It comes into the hearts of men.

All flesh is then consumed.

Only the awe of God remains.

The awe of God tarries,

to burn,

to spread,

to grow.

Chapter 18

RENEWAL

My Old Self says,

"I hate you.

You're not worthy of love.

You've made too many bad
mistakes!"

Father says,

"I love you.

I made you in My image.

My love makes you whole."

My New Self says,

"I love you.

You ARE worthy.

I forgive you. You ARE whole."

I John 4:13-19

Chapter 18

THE WASHING

In the soft glow of the fireplace, He beckons me to come near and snuggle beside Him on the couch—in that hidden place of safety and acceptance.

His voice radiates kindness. "You're afraid you have made a mistake, aren't you?"

I nod, shoulders hunched and eyes closed, afraid to meet His gaze. "Now what happens, Lord?"

"What happens is that I keep on loving you, my little one." He smiles. "It doesn't matter so much whether you made a mistake or not. What matters is that you feel dirty, shamed and guilty at even the possibility that you might have made a wrong decision."

"You mean I don't have to be perfect" (Rom. 8:15)?

"No, you don't. Let me explain. When a little boy comes back to his daddy all covered with mud, it doesn't concern him so much how his son got dirty. He just cleans him up and loves him." Slow, gentle words.

"I do the same. For it is love that anchors My heart. It is unending, unlimited and unedited. Love is the pulsating heartbeat of God, streaming into the open cracks of the wounded human heart. I rejoice in the healing of them all. Don't keep beating up yourself. Always come to Me first. Never allow anything to remain between us as an irritant. A festering sore will eat at our relationship and erect a wall. Over time, it will grow huge in your imagination."

I know exactly what He means. My thoughts swing back to years long past. As a young woman, I desperately prayed for the restoration of a most important relationship. When it did not happen, I became angry with God. Yes, I did put up a wall to separate myself from Him. Subconsciously, I thought, *I'll show Him. I'll get even with Him.* Little did I realize that I was hurting myself. I was the one left wandering for years in the desert of life. When I finally stopped pushing Him away, allowing Him to touch my cold heart, He thawed the anger in an instant. Down came the wall and out went all unforgiveness, resentment and grief. My hope was revived, and I could again praise Him (Is. 61:3 RSV). With a slight shake of my head, I bring my thoughts back to the present to focus on Him.

With tenderness He says, "Now come. Hand Me all the dirtiness. First the guilt and then the shame. As you release it into My river of forgiveness, I wash it away and make you clean again. It's as simple as that. I dress your heart in the heavenly cloak of peace, and I just love you."

My heart leaps at the invitation, and I allow
Him to heal me in His way. He holds me close for a
long time. My heart melts within me at so great a
love and so thorough a washing. No self-
condemnation remains (Rom. 8:1). It is a gift
beyond all imagination…to be clean, to be loved
and to know that nothing will ever separate me from
the love of my Father (Rom. 8:38-39).

Chapter 18

THE HEART OF THE FATHER

Be still.

Do you feel it?

Are you aware of the magnetic draw...

the inexorable pull into the center of life,

the center of the pulsating heart of the Father,

the heart from which you sprang,

the heart of love?

Be still.

Do you feel it?

Can you sense it?

*It beats with the rhythm of
life.*

It yearns for you,

for your return.

*The heart of the Father, set
by default,*

*set to the continual ticking of
the hands of*

eternity...

drawing,

tugging,

*pulling you back into the
heart of love.*

Stop.

Stop all resistance.

Allow yourself to be drawn home

into the arms of love.

Job 14:15 NIV

Chapter 19

THE WATER OF LIFE

Take hold of life, hang on tight.

Life is Him, it flows from Him.

He is the water of Life, the river of Life.

Enter the water...

Give way to the water.

Go deeper

And deeper

And deeper in Him...

Until you are one in Him

And He in you.

One and the same.

Chapter 19

THE WATERFALL

There is an air of expectation about Him that I have not noticed before. The Bridegroom takes my hand, and together we stroll the winding pathways of the garden until we come upon an abrupt turn, hidden from public view. There in the distance is a majestic cascading waterfall. The shimmering water dances its way from the rocky heights to the refreshing river winding down the flowered slopes of grace.

In admiration I sit on the large sun warmed bench to take in the beauty of it. He takes his rightful position close beside me. In a most purposeful way, He quietly begins sharing His love.

"I come to you in the stillness of the deep (Ps. 62:5). I come revealing myself to you in My perfect Word (Ps. 19:7-10). I come knocking at your door in the midnight hour when there is only calmness within your soul (Ps. 131:2). In the quietness I sink deep inside you. The weight of My Presence unlocks heart areas which before were inaccessible (Song.of Sg. 5:4). There is where My reality settles itself as truth within you" (Eph. 4:21), and we become one in spirit (I Cor. 6:17).

My breathing quickens and becomes shallow.

"But this is different," He continues. "As we come here, one in spirit to the roaring onrush of My streaming glory (Ps. 43:6b), eagerness and excitement rise within Me. Here I am not contained or restrained in My expression of love for you. Here I can roar as a lion within the thunderous noise of rushing water (Rev. 1:15). Here, as a lamb, I can touch you with the spray of mist on your skin. Here I can carry to you on waterdrops the kisses of my love (Job 36:27-28). Here you catch the fresh scent of Me and the pure taste of Me. In the sparkling sunlight you gather glimpses of the glory light radiating from Me. I fill all in all (Eph. 1:23). My presence is everywhere" (Ps. 139:6-12).

I realize He is opening to me the recesses of His heart as never before. My thoughts spin, and my breathing pauses at the marvel of it all (Rom. 11:33-34).

"I can reveal Myself to you in a myriad of ways through the medium of creation (Ps. 19:1-4). Nature is the brush in My hand as I paint My reality on the canvas of your soul. The stars display My infinity; the smoothness of a baby's skin, My tenderness; the colors of a sunset, My glory; lamb's wool, glistening and soft, My hair (Rev.1:14); the heat of a campfire, My love; the brilliance of a diamond, My purity.

"Stop resisting (Acts 7:51). That's all you need to do. Let your spirit come alive with the understanding that I am totally enraptured with you, My Bride. You will find that the world will also come tingling back to life for you in the realization of how much you are loved."

The rising truth of His words begins to bubble to the surface of my consciousness, and I do drop all resistance.

"Take My hand now. When you are ready, we will walk as one into that waterfall. There My love will flow over, in and through you to fill and refresh your empty, parched soul. Remember, My love will never deplete you. It will always nourish you (John 15:9). There, in the waters, we will enter the secret place where Bride and Bridegroom come together in spirit, rejoicing and singing. There we will surrender ourselves to each other, and there you will 'Fasten Me upon your heart as a seal of fire forevermore. This living, consuming flame will seal you as My prisoner of love. My passion is stronger than the chains of death and the grave, all-consuming as the very flashes of fire from the burning heart of God. Place this fierce, unrelenting fire over your entire being.'" (Song of Sg. 8:6).

In joyous confidence I begin walking forward with Him into freedom and life. The expectation of what lies ahead fills us as the cascading waters pull us together in free fall into the limitless depths of the magnitude of the astonishing love of God (Eph. 3:18-19).

Chapter 19

FREE

*Free...I'm free in the Water of
Life.*

Anchors are cut,

tethers are loosed,

shackles are off.

I'm free...I'm free

to float and twirl,

to dance, to sing,

to leap and dive,

to be...to be me!

I'm free...I'm free

to explore the depths of the riches
of God,

to explode in the air with the
glory of God,

to expand my heart with the
presence of God,

to expel the foe with the power of
God.

Chapter 20

THE KEY

TO

B

E

I

N

G

*

Inexorably,

We allow ourselves to be drawn

In ever tightening circles

Into the presence of

LOVE

HIMSELF—

Until with abandon

All resistance

Ceases,

And we

Become

ONE.

Chapter 20

THE UNION

Upon waking the next morning in the stillness of Him, I find myself wondering, *What shall I do now as I go forward? What's next?*

I hear the familiar voice of the Teacher (Is. 30:20-21) within me begin speaking, "You will find within you an ever-deepening sense of oneness with Me (Song of Sg. 6:3)…no more separation or distinction between the two of us—similar to a married couple who has only grown more in love as the years have gone by. They cherish one another. Each is mindful of the other. They think the same; each anticipates the reactions of the other. They are aware of every changing nuance. There is such a knowing of and safety in one another that they move and think as one. There is total acceptance, understanding and honor. The union that began years ago with the covenant of marriage has now become totally complete in all areas of their lives."

I can hear the smile in His voice. "So it is with us. This is where the fullness of God becomes powerful as it overflows into lives around you (Eph. 3:19). It is natural. There is nothing forced or tainted about our unity (Song of Sg. 8:14). There is no longer a striving for love, acceptance or attention. You know you already have it. With total faith you can rest securely in Me."

My heart settles down into peace as I hear His words of assurance (Heb. 4:8-11). Now I'm drawn to listen with even more attention.

"From such a position in Me the living waters of My Spirit can flow unhindered, releasing the sufficiency of Myself into whomever or whatever situation may arise (John 7:38-39). Because we are one, I will flow from the place of rest within you—no effort on your part. There will be an anointing of ease you have now only begun to experience. Who you really are will come forth (Col. 3:4) in creativity, power and fruit (Song of Sg. 4:13-14).

"Creativity is a gift which mirrors Me. I see in it an expression of Myself. When you create something original, it brings honor to Me; and in the process of that creativity, you are drawn into union with Me (Col. 3:4). You sense My nearness as we walk in collaboration. That is what gives you a passion for whatever I have gifted you to do."

He pauses to give me time to absorb His words and then continues. "Don't fight it. Give way to it. Go with the flow of My Spirit (Col. 2:6) to release new expressions of both Myself and you into the world. Just as people 'ooh and aah' at the sight of a newborn baby, they will marvel at My reflection in what has come forth from you. What they see in you will nurture them in the ways of the Kingdom of God" (Song of Sg. 4:5).

A look of deep satisfaction lights up His face.

"You have allowed yourself to be merged into oneness with My Spirit. You function well as a part of the body of Christ even as your own individual personality shines through. You are a brilliant facet of that body when in union with Me.

"In answer to your question, I will tell you what is next." His bright smile encourages my heart. "With enthusiasm and confidence, we will go forward together (Rom. 15:17) into the passionate adventure that is life."

Chapter 20

BREAK OUT

Break out...
out of your shell,
your shell so dark and hard.

There's more...
more out there,
of which you're yet unaware.

There's freedom...
freedom to be,
who God meant you to be.

Break in…

into life,

into light.

Now, walk…

Walk in life,

in light.

Walk in Him.

*"Life came into being because of
Him,*

*For His life is light for all
humanity."*

John 1:4

Chapter 21

WHEN

When you walk through the
shadows

And grief rolls o'er your soul,

The Man of Sorrows whispers,
"Fear not.

You'll again be whole."

When you walk through the fire

And the flames blaze hot,

The Lord of Hosts thunders,
"Fear not.

I am here."

When you walk through the
waters

And all your strength
disappears,

The great I AM declares, "Fear
not.

I am near."

When you walk through hope
deferred

And there is not a star in sight,

The Lord of Glory tells you, "Fear
not.

I am light."

Isaiah 43:1-2

Chapter 21

THE KNOCK

Fear comes knocking at the door.

My mind races in that direction, but I choose not to answer. Instead, I turn quickly to the One joined to my heart. (Prov. 18:24). He ignores the knock. With the tenderness of a shepherd, He leads me away from the door to divert my attention.

"What are you afraid of?"

I fall weeping at His feet, my heart broken.

"Just anything and everything, it seems like. I feel like a failure. I want to stand strong against fear. I can do it for a while. Then it just slips in again, and I'm back where I started. I don't know what to do."

In between sobs, tears continue to stream down my face.

"I've walked with You for a long time, yet I'm just not standing firm in this—in how to be bigger than my fear. Please teach me, Lord. I want to trust You. I want to learn from You because You know all things. I don't want to be afraid anymore. Help me."

The floor beneath my face is wet with tears, but suddenly I perceive a subtle shift in the atmosphere. I open my eyes to find myself face down in velvety grass. Lifting my head, I soon realize I am back in the fields of grace.

"What is going on?" I wonder.

I sense His presence changing. I no longer see His earthly sandals. His feet now gleam like bright metal glowing in a fire (Rev.1:15).

All fear vanishes. My racing heart is calmed; my tears and sobs stilled. Instead, a holy awe begins to spread throughout my entire being. My circumstances remain in the background, but their existence is now overridden by a Presence greater than all else.

I look up from the grass and hesitantly bring myself up to my knees, not knowing what awaits. One glance of the King of all kings, burning with the brightness of the blinding sun, drops me again to the ground. I am totally undone.

Time passes. I know not how long until again I hear the voice of the Teacher above me in the house. He takes my hand, lifting me to my feet.

"You have just seen with your eyes the answer to your question. You have seen me as I really am. Don't yield to fear (Rev. 1:17-18). There will always be fear and trouble in this world (Job 5:7 NIV). When you return to your vision of Me in all My glory and power, those distractions will no longer have any grip on you. You will be able to focus on Me, and all else will fade into unimportance—even pain. That's how you live in Me. Even though your body exists here on this earthly plane, you can keep the eyes of your spirit consciously or unconsciously fixed on Me."

My heart melts into His as His steady gaze infuses me with strength. Words my mother used to sing come to mind…the chorus of a hymn by Helen Lemmel: "Turn your eyes upon Jesus: Look full in His wonderful face, And the things of earth will grow strangely dim, In the light of His glory and grace."

I have made you strong for such a time as this," He reminds me. Even though you may doubt your ability to endure, My imprint is on your life. I have made you as steel refined in the fire. As you believe that, it will become reality within you.

The next time you hear a fearful knock, turn your eyes toward Me. Keep them there for as long as needed. Future knocks will come, but they'll no longer sound as loud. When concentrating on Who I've revealed Myself to be, you will perceive these knocks as only light taps. Before you even realize it, you will be the conqueror not fear.

Chapter 21

REST

Come and rest.
Lean your head on Me.
Settle your thoughts,
Nestle your heart in Me.

Come and rest.
Release your yoke to Me.
Cease from cares,
Receive joy from Me.

Come and rest.
Cease from stress with Me.
Release your fears,

Receive peace from Me.

Come and rest.
Change will cease to be
A fear to thee
As we walk upon the sea.

Come and rest in Me.

Chapter 22

SWEPT

Swept along

Swept along by the Spirit—

Lifted by the Spirit

*Lifted by the Spirit to
dizzying heights*

*Where the natural and the
supernatural seem to*

*blend...blending the heart and
the spirit of man*

Until

*He becomes one spirit with the
Spirit of Emmanuel*

*And together all things become
possible...*

Chapter 22

THE LIVING WORD

"Go to the well. Go to the well."

In the early morning hours, these words echoing in my heart carry a vague familiarity. I hesitate to leave to leave the cozy warmth of my blanketed bed but feel I must answer this call of mystery. I arise, slip on some clothes and make my way through dew-soaked grass to the well. The eastern sky is set ablaze with the fiery colors of dawn. The faint scent of lilac captivates my senses.

Coming near the stone well, I find on the hard ground an old-fashioned wooden bucket with clear, fresh water. Submerged in its midst is a glass baby bottle…half filled with milk. A surge of wonder swells up within me. Pulling it out, I remember the days before refrigeration. As a little bitty girl, I would sometimes toddle my way over to the old windmill in the center of the farmyard. With Sheppie, our collie dog, beside me, I would retrieve my milk—yes, stored in a pail filled with cold water.

Beside me the King would be the only one still having knowledge of this.

The cherished memories of the past are clear, and the bottle still dripping wet as I press it close to me. There is a pause in time; but, just on the edge of my awareness, I sense the coldness fading. A warmth spreads across my hands. Looking down in amazement, I see a wondrous transformation. It's a God thing. That's the only way to explain it.

Next to my heart now is a soft, brown leather Bible with a narrow strip of embossed intertwining circles and squares. The season has switched, and I've become a big girl holding in my hands the nourishing milk of the Word (I Cor. 3:2). It is literally pulsating with life. It's not an inanimate book. It is the Word of the King Himself (John 1:1).

I am clueless about how to respond, but I do know this Word is life itself. Without it my spirit will shrivel and die. Instinctively, I realize this is my God-breathed connection to Father. It's my all in all. I enfold it in both my arms and hold it next to my heart as if to never let it go.

As I do this, I feel the Living Expression of the Word (John 1:1) being absorbed into my inner being and becoming solid food (Heb. 5:11-14), the ultimate manna to every cell of my body (1 Cor. 10:3-4). It refreshes, strengthens and nourishes my soul. The Light of Truth (John 1:9) reflected from the pages begins to burn within my heart (Luke 24:32).

While pondering this marvel, I'm aware I have not only opened the lid of the treasure chest of His Word, His very Self; but I have allowed myself to be drawn into it. I discover layer upon layer of spiritual riches. I feast on heavenly realities (Col. 3:2), admiring each strand of pearly peace, each ruby love bracelet and the emerald necklaces of joy and abundance. I take time for the images to forever be imprinted in my memory.

As I delve into the wonder of the Word, I realize it is bottomless. I abandon all caution and permit myself to plumb the depths of the burning heart of Love Himself. An envelopment of peace ushers me downward to the glowing coals (Is. 6:6). At the core of His being I lay, a living sacrifice, on the altar of His heart, purified to burn as a holy blue flame—for Him, in Him and with Him. I am at one with Him in His glory (Col.3:4).

Chapter 22

YOUR FIRE

Ignite Your fire in me.

Melt me.

Purify me.

*Pour me into the mold You have
shaped for me,*

*To be the vessel You've always
seen me to be...*

*A vessel pouring out the
consuming fire of You,*

The light and hope of You,

The love of You,

For eternity...

Lost in You.

Chapter 23

THE GRAND MASTERPIECE

We've come nearer to the end of
the road

And see the grand plan unfold...

The hurts, pains, sorrows and
joys,

The bitterness, the sweetness

The partings, joinings,

The mistakes, the corrections,

The staleness, freshness...

All fitting together as strokes of
the brush

In the hand of the Great Creator.

"And it was good."

Genesis 1:12b

Chapter 23

THE FATHER

I am having a full-blown temper tantrum. I have just pushed away the spiritual ladle of blessings my Father was ready to pour for me. I am upset with Him, myself and my friend who is moving far away to start a new chapter of her life.

With my fists I beat on His chest in anger. "Why are you doing this, Father? Why are You taking her away? She's my friend!"

Setting all else aside, He walks to the small guest room, coming back with my mother's velvet-lined jewelry box. Inside is one of Mom's treasures. She had safely stored it for seventy-six of her ninety-eight years. It was a gold necklace my father had sent her when he was stationed abroad during World War II. An ornately engraved locket dangles from it. Nestled inside are pictures of them both, young and so in love with life and with each other.

Father begins to speak. "She held it tightly to herself. Yes, it was hers. Yes, she treasured it. But now it has become tarnished, and very few others have been able to appreciate it. How much better to have brought it out to be seen. It would have shone and sparkled in the light. Its beauty would've been shared. It would have brought genuine admiration to the hearts of family and friends.

"So it is with the people or things we value. If we do not share them, they discolor in the darkness or don't reach their full potential. However, if the lockets of our hearts are opened to the sun, our treasures are unfettered and become a joy to many. People will see My light reflected from them and give Me glory. Whatever you release to Me will shine with My brilliance.

"Keeping the blessing of someone to yourself can be likened to this. Picture a couple of young lion cubs playing with and enjoying one another in the dim light of the den where they were born. The lioness knows that this is good for a time, but now there is much awaiting her young ones—more horizons to see, adventures to have and situations to conquer. By the scruff of their necks, she picks them up one by one and carries them out into the sunlight of the world around them. There they can grow into their full identities. New challenges, exploits and victories lie ahead. They will both become strong, yet they will still continue to build up one another and defeat common enemies."

"I understand, Father," I quietly reply. "Only as I release my prized possessions into Your hands, will they become the objects of beauty you have always intended them to be. You've said, 'In Thy presence is fullness of joy, in Thy right hand are pleasures for evermore' (Ps. 16:1 RSV). Only as I relinquish to You what I considered 'Mine, mine,' will I be able to receive the greatest treasure of all—You.

"I forgive myself, Lord. I forgive You. I forgive my friend."

I pause, allowing my heart time to absorb all that Father has shared. Eventually, it dawns on me that the sun has just filled my heart (Ps.90:14). I feel so light, like I could just take off and fly like a bird.

With a grin, I turn toward Him. "I am ready. I'm ready now to receive that ladle of love, life and abundance…that overflow of You (Ps. 36:7-9).

"As I keep taking in all the good You have for me, let me become strong and healthy, inside and out. Let me grow up to be just like You, Father, like You originally meant me to be."

His eyes smile down at me, and His grin broadens.

"You will. You will be just as I saw you before the world ever began-a brilliant light in this world-reflecting Me." (II Cor. 4:6-7).

Chapter 23

THE FATHER'S VOICE

Come near.

Come near Me in the stillness.

No fear.

I long to hear the beating of your
heart next to Mine,

to feel your presence near Me,

to share My love's overflow with
you.

In the silence

My essence is absorbed like dew

into the very fiber of your being.

A hunger arises within you...

a yearning

a longing for more.

Earth's vanities fade

in the vibrancy of My song over you

for I am the fiery core of life itself.

Come to the core; come to Me.

I am your Father.

I take delight in you.

You are made in My image, reflecting Me;

You bear My stamp of approval:

'Made in Heaven.'

I claim you.

You are Mine.
I love you.

Chapter 24

THE TRANSFORMATION

The Old Creature,
marred and scarred—
Holy Spirit come...
remove all darkness and sin,
make my heart pure within,
uncover the deceit deep therein,
to show that alone, I cannot win.

The cloud of original sin
has stained all within.
Only Your blood will undo the
damage therein.

To the altar Self is consigned,

drawn there at just the right
time.

It must yield to its own death

and give up its last breath.

BUT...

"Death is swallowed up in
victory.

Death, where is your sting?

Grave, where is your victory?"

Up from the grave He arose

With a mighty victory o'er His
foes...

And so I arise...

The New Creation,

Unmarred and unscarred—

Holy Spirit come...

fill me with light and right,

keep my heart pure within,

covered with truth deep therein

*to show that with Him, I can
win.*

I Cor. 15:54-55

Rom. 8:37

THE ENCOUNTER

I am standing at the kitchen table, minding my own business. Out of nowhere comes His unmistakable voice speaking within. "I am of purer eyes than to behold evil" (Hab. 1:13 RSV). Words I learned years ago were now coming to life within me. "The soul that sins shall die" (Ez. 18:4b RSV).

I freeze. I know this is me. My trembling body, my thumping heart and my burning chest all betray me.

I am in the presence of a Holy God. Guilty as charged.

I fall on my face, tears streaming onto the cold vinyl floor beneath my cheeks.

"Have mercy on me, or I will die." My heart is filled with terror. This is an encounter with the Living God! This is a side of Him I have never seen before, only read about—the stark reality of the awe filled holiness of God. I truly do not know if I will survive.

"Wash me, O God. Make my heart clean. My sin, oh my sin. It is so great. Purify me."

A flashing ray of light sparks within my numbed brain. *"Only one hope I have…the blood.* "One drop," I gasp. "Just one, one will save me." I despair of life itself. This is the first time I have seen my appearance through His eyes. "I am so defiled." It was not that I had done anything horribly wrong. It was just that, in the sight of a holy God, even one lie would move me into the guilty category.

The next words forcing their way to the surface of my memory are "Nothing in my hand I bring; simply to Thy cross I cling." How often had I sung that song snuggled next to my mom in the old white country church near our farm. From the look on my dad's face whenever we sang that hymn, I somehow knew he cherished those words. Now I feel them embedded also in my heart.

"I am of unclean lips and an unclean heart" (Is. 6:5-6 RSV). Those words echo in the chambers of my heart. *I cannot exist like this in the presence of a holy God. My life is hanging in the balance. I must change. I need to do something.*

"Create in me a clean heart, O God" (Ps. 51:10). Again, words cemented into the fabric of time long past.

I somehow bring my trembling knees under me and crawl to the fridge. Grabbing on to the handle, I expend my last ounce of strength to bring myself to a standing position. *I must get out bread and the wine. My life depends on it. Why is this happening, Lord?*

My shaking hands seem to have lost all contact with my brain, but I retrieve the treasure for which I am searching. Collapsing on the nearby kitchen chair, I barely manage to bring to my open mouth His body broken for me, and His blood shed for me. I find the power of that blood stands unchallenged. It is as effective now as the day it was first shed. It flows through my heart's door and back in time—down the stained ancestral blood line of my generations, cleansing as it goes. It is followed by the explosive power of Holy Spirit's glory light, healing all soul wounds before returning and nestling again in the hidden place of my heart.

The heavenly voice declares, "It is finished (John 19:30), for time and eternity."

His precious blood has cleansed my heart and lips. The work is done. I see myself now from a different perspective—dressed in the pure white linen of His righteousness—faultless to stand before the throne.

Exhausted and drained of all energy, I fall fast asleep with my head on the kitchen table. I rest for a long while in the peace of forgiveness.

Eventually I bestir myself, sitting up to find that I have not been alone. Watching over me all the while, my Shepherd King has stayed at my side. In the nearness of His presence I feel my heartstrings being pulled toward Him. In faith, I drop all resistance and find my spirit poured out, melted into Him with such a loving flow that separation becomes a thing of the past. Remaining, is a pure oneness of being, of purpose and movement…an unstoppable stream of Him flowing through me with such abandon that I can barely contain the sweep of it.

My spirit is not only caught up with Him, but also rooted in Him as the very source of my existence (Eph. 3:17-20). The fiery flames in our hearts merge to burn as one in the purified atmosphere of love. I am well. I am complete. I am whole.

Chapter 24

FIRE

Burning flames of fire,
Purifying, electrifying
Burning flames of fire.

Come, Spirit of the Living God,
Burn away the dross
Set on fire the cross
Emblazoned on our thoughts.

Let us burn for You,
Holy
Wholly true
To You and only You.

Chapter 25

THE GRAND ADVENTURE

Tis a grand adventure we are on,

In time we will finish strong.

The path ahead we cannot see,

But have no fear—to Him it's
clear.

The past is gone, it's over...done.

Leave it there...go on, go on.

It can drag you down, you see,

And keep you from all you're
meant to be.

The future lies ahead.

We know not how it will be
spread,

But through the day and every
night

We know...He will be our light.

Chapter 25

THE NARROW PLACE

I sit relaxing on the broad white veranda in the early morning hours. It has become one of my favorite spots in the hidden place. With a hot cup of honey flavored lemon tea warming my hands, I lift my gaze to the rocky peaks and mountain ledges highlighted in the snowy distance. So far and yet so close.

Will I ever get to go there or experience what I once imagined life would be? Will I still be able to have the adventure of crossing over to the other side?

I lower my glance from the dream of the heights to the clothes I find myself wearing. The sympathetic voice of my dear Friend (Ex. 33:11a RSV) lounging beside me brings reality into even sharper focus.

"Are you wondering how you will ever manage to squeeze through those tight, narrow places up there while wearing your roughly hewn cloak of humility?

He always knows and understands my every thought (Ps. 139:3-4).

"This is how your cloak appears to the proud eyes of the enemy, but he cannot see beneath the surface. He doesn't realize that inside is a luxurious, soft purple lining, soothing to the touch. The enemy forces look down on humility and treat it with contempt (Prov. 15:33; 22:4 RSV). It is of no value to them. It is to be despised and rejected, having no redeeming qualities."

A smile lights up His face.

"I do not look on outward appearances, but at what is happening inside (I Sam.16:7 RSV). Within that cloak of humility a metamorphosis is taking place, such as within the cocoon of a butterfly. Your heart is being molded and shaped into My image until you come forth as a new creation (II Cor. 5:17 RSV). Your new self will slip with ease through any tight place. You will have been transformed into My likeness in the fire (Is. 48:10 RSV) and in the waters of affliction (Is. 43:1-2 RSV)."

Noticing my furrowed brow, He continues.

"There remains no longer any Velcro of the world, the flesh and the devil on or within you (I John 2:15-17)…nothing in common with the evil one (John 14:30 KJV). In My river of life you become almost fluid like, being able to flow through situations which would have before been too sticky. Do not be deceived, as the enemy is, by the cloak of humility. It is most powerful in my arsenal of weapons (Matt. 18:1-4).

And by the way, don't try to take anyone else with you through your narrow place in the spirit. Your passageway will not resemble that of another's. Each child of mine has his own unique blend of attributes, background and temptations. What is a challenge or testing for you will not necessarily be a difficulty for others in the body of Christ. Each must pass through his narrow place in his own way and in his own time, with no baggage of any kind.

You will meet your friends again on the other side—all of you stronger and wiser than before. Be bold; be strong and courageous (Josh.1:9 NIV). Together then, under My banner (Song of Sg. 2:4), you will face the giants of the land in the grandest adventure of all. You will not be on defense but on offense. The angels of heaven will fight with you. Great will be your victory."

Reaching out, He takes my hand, lifting me to my feet. As we begin dancing to the rhythm of the silence around us, the birds take up the chorus and the outer roughness of my cloak is folded inward, disappearing into the beauty of the truth that lies within.

Chapter 25

VICTORY

The days that come will be great
days of victory.

Darkness falls upon the earth,
It crackles with My kingdom's
birth.
Kings will rise and kings will fall
Yet My power conquers all.

Do not fear, but heed the call,
Obey my voice above all.
Love and light will prevail,
My presence will not fail.

*Come to Me. We'll go forth in
victory.*

JOURNEY OF THE WILL

*I growled. I hissed. I spat like a
wild, scared alley cat—*

*a hand extended in love...
"Come."*

*I growled. I hissed like a wild
alley cat—*

*a hand extended in love...
"Come."*

I growled like an alley cat—

*a hand extended in love...
"Come."*

I studied that hand like a hungry
cat—

a hand extended in love...
"Come."

I submitted to that hand like a
loved cat.

I purred in that hand like a
contented cat—

a hand extended in love...
"Home. You're home."

Chapter 26

THE WILL

The searing pain in my body has been here since Sunday afternoon. This is now Tuesday evening. The knife stabbing sensation is beginning its third night of keeping me tossing and turning, with but a week until Christmas.

In desperation I cry out, "Lord, help me. Please help me" (Ps. 109:26).

In answer, He immediately opens the eyes of my heart (Eph. 1:18) to see my stubborn will as He does—an immovable upright column.

My brows knit together as I wonder, *What does this have to do with the pain in my body?*

I watch as He applies the blazing fire of His love to the rigid beam. Like a blow torch, it is focused on the center of that unrelenting will. I am shocked to see that it corresponds exactly to the epicenter of the stiffening pain I have been feeling. The correlation is undeniable.

The heat grows more intense until I see my will glowing red hot and melting into a river of molten lava.

"Lord, there's nothing left of me," I cry out.

At that precise moment the truth explodes within me.

"Oh-h-h my. That has been Your intention all the while, hasn't it? Less of me and more of You. Not my will but Thine be done" (Luke 22:42).

In regret, my thoughts flash back to one of many times in my life when I wanted to have my way, not being sensitive to anyone else.

It was summer, and I was driving home with my family after vacationing in Canada. I had insisted on taking the long route through Glacier Park even though I knew my dad was lethargic from little sleep and much pain. He had a pillow clutched to his tummy the whole way back. Soon after we returned, he ended up in the hospital with a ruptured appendix. He almost died. That was a hard lesson to learn.

And yet, one still not fully learned.

I'm saddened to realize my thinking has wandered for so many years down the path of self will. *I'm my own boss. I'll do what I want to do.*

It's turned into an unconscious habit of resistance…until a few days ago. In one unforgettable scene from a dream, He brings me up short. I see myself playing the role of a bridesmaid in His wedding. But I am not the bride. I'm cut to the quick. My heart is broken.

"No, no, Lord," I cry. "Let it not be so. Give me another chance. Being Your bride is the deepest yearning of my heart. Please, fix me."

The scene changes, and there He is…the Bridegroom Himself. He is standing before me in all tenderness and purity. At first glance I know I am forgiven.

With inviting eyes of love, He calls to me, "Come. Come, My Bride."

I walk directly into His heart. As the double doors close behind me, there is only peace. Total undisturbed peace within that hidden place. I am drawn into the depths of Him. I see the place where the burning lava of my will has been absorbed into His fiery river of passionate love.

Later, as we sit relaxing down near the bank, I realize my heart is once again pliable in His hands. Furthermore, to my great delight, my body also is loosed to move pain free.

As I give myself permission to think about what has just happened, He takes my hands. In a soft voice He begins answering the questions in my mind.

"You truly had yielded to Me before, but only in part, only as much as you cared to. This time was different. Since you've grown to know Me better, you've learned to trust Me more. So today you felt comfortable enough to give Me unrestricted access. Earlier you would have considered that part of yourself off limits. You would've guarded it as your sole domain. However, when I see a heart in readiness, I'm always eager to move forward with the good work I started in it long ago" (Phil. 1:6).

I nod, beginning to understand. "As I allow myself to merge with You, Your will empowers me; it does not weaken me. Together with You I can become all You originally created me to be."

I am moved to lift my voice in adoration and praise of the Most High King (Ps. 47:2). In my spirit I see the golden doors of heaven swing open to a Christmas celebration. For a brief time and a short distance, I can join my new song (Ps. 96:1) with those of the choirs of heaven in procession to the city of God, the Holy Place of the Lord God Almighty. I blend my voice with theirs in adoration of the babe of Bethlehem, the Lord of Lords, the King of Kings (Rev. 17-14), the Holy One who was and is and is to come (Rev. 4:8).

FIX IT, DADDY

Running...
Running to my daddy,
Tears of distress streaming down
my face—
Broken toy in hand,
"Daddy, Daddy, fix it please."

Returning...
Returning to my dad...
Broken heart in hand,
Tears of sorrow streaming down
my face—
"Dad, oh dad, fix it please."

Remaining...

Remaining with my Father...

Healed heart in hand,

Tears of joy streaming down my face—

Father, You have fixed it. Thank you.

You have made me whole."

Chapter 27

I AM

You are closer than the air I breathe.

How can that be?

I AM the air you breathe.

I AM the breath you take.

I AM life itself.

"And God breathed…and Adam became a living being."

Gen.2:7 NIV

I AM the beginning and the end.

I AM the Alpha and the Omega.

I inhabit every cell of your being.

And yet...

I AM larger than life itself.

Exodus 3:14 RSV

Chapter 27

THE SONGS IN THE NIGHT

The night is pregnant with love, and it's a time of birthing…a birthing of hope, of expectations not yet met, of dreams faded with time, of glory yet to come. The time is now. Let it be—the passion of the ages coming forth in the deep recesses of the secret place (Ps. 32:7). The water breaks; the flood gates open; eternity breaks through the web of earth to mesh in tremors of love (Song of Sg. 5:4b).

In the close stillness of the night my overflowing heart senses His presence draw near. At His touch the dam breaks. In the mutual spillover of joy the love songs stream over our lips. They cannot be contained; they must be shared, one with another.

"You are the One my heart loves, my King. You are my all in all. In You I have everything; without You I have nothing. You are my treasure, my tower, my bed of flowers" (Prov. 18:10).

"Come. Come to Me," is His lyrical response. "My arms enfold you with the whisper of love. My heart thrills to your face lifted to Mine in trust. My ears are attuned to the melody of My breath blowing through the chimes of your spirit. My eyes soak in your hunger for more of Me.

"Come, My dove, My little one. I will hold and care for you in your weakness, but I will also empower you to fly in joyful exhilaration. You will catch the current of My Spirit as it lifts you into realms of delight. For this you were created—to explore the height, depths and riches of My love for you. As you spread your wings and soar, you will embody My Spirit. You'll come forth from your cocoon, bearing My image and spreading My scent" (II Cor. 2:14-16).

"All I've ever wanted was to be loved." The yearning softness of my voice betrays me, but my honesty is matched by His.

"All I've ever wanted was to be loved too—and to love you."

"I am made in Your image, Lord" (Gen. 1:26).

"Yes, you are. Your desire to be loved mirrors Mine. Taste and see that I am good (Ps. 34:8 RSV). I am the Good Shepherd Who lays down His life for the sheep (John 10:11). Your hungry heart mirrors Mine. See for yourself. Peer into the depths of My soul. Don't be afraid. Look."

"I see only shimmering pools of love, My King, that span all of eternity."

"Come. Come closer. Breathe deeply of Me. Allow the fire of My love to ignite your soul to sing

My praises. Let your passion for Me exceed your passion for life.

"Call out. Call out in the night, and I will come to you with my hair wet with dew (Song of Sg. 5:2, footnote). I'll unlock the door of your heart (Song of Sg. 5:4a), and I will enter…"

"Stop." My burning thirst for Him interrupts. "Gather me in Your arms; wrap me in Your love. Lead me into that bliss of being face-to-face with You" (Ps. 16:11).

"Yes, come quickly My precious one. Let Me envelop you in My goodness. Let My Spirit within raise you to new vistas of color, vibrancy and love…into My presence, My joy and yours forevermore."

Chapter 27

THE ENVELOPING

The Spirit's Approach: so gentle,
tender and slow…

like

a glint of light on a rock below

the hint of color near the dawn of
the morn

His rainbow in the sky after the
storm

The rays of heat on a hot
summer's day…

all speak and all say,

"I seek entrance…

into your life…

into your day.

Will you let Me in to love you My
way?"

"Yes," you say.

The Spirit's Entrance: so gentle,
tender and slow…

like

a mist in the morning He enters
in,

with a smile settling Himself way
down low

to fill your being with a deep,
deep peace…

to give your life a brand-new
lease.

The Spirit's Love: so gentle,
tender and subtle…

as

a scent of perfume in a room

a trickling of warm water over
the toes

a gradual unfolding of the petals
of a rose

a shimmer of light in a garden of
delight

a faint tinkling of bells far over
the knell

a choice of a breeze on a warm
summer's eve

a taste of honey entering your
tummy...

the soft presence of Your Spirit in
mine.

"Be still and know that I AM
God."

Psalm 46:10

Chapter 28

SONG OF SONGS

Come and dance with Me to
the rhythm of My soul.

Trust and yield to Me the
core of your soul.

Come and soar with Me.

Feel the flow of Me in your
rhythm of life…

pulsating with the sweet
perfume of love

to the tune of the song of all
songs!

Chapter 28

THE HIGH PLACES

"Come with Me to the high places," is His unexpected invitation.

My eyes widen in surprise. My heart is both leaping and sinking at the same time. I take a quick glance at the slopes leading in that direction. The dried, pale grass is barely peeking through the light covering of fresh snow. The air is cool and crisp. Paths leading to the purple hued peaks could be slippery this time of year. *Am I ready?* I wonder. *Can I do this? What will it be like?*

In a quick burst of courage, I drop my fear at His feet. I have learned in the hidden place that I can choose to ignore the doubts. I know, now, I can trust Him with my heart. I fix my gaze on the steady strength reflected from His eyes (Heb. 12:2). My hand, joining His in a firm grip, anchors me in security and imparts boldness to my voice.

"Okay, I'm ready to go with You."

With a grin He replies, "You've just been there."

"What?" I stare at Him. "I don't understand.

The delight in His smile matches the twinkle in His eyes.

"You tend to think of the high places as somewhere far away and unattainable, but they reside within your heart. Every time you push doubts aside and choose trust, you have been to the heights (Ps. 18:33). Every time you grasp My hand, instead of the hand of fear, you have conquered new plateaus. Since they are found within, each person has his or her own unique challenges (Hab. 3:19 NIV). Each time you choose to trust Me in a new area, with a less hesitant manner or a quicker response, I am pleased. You are learning to use your hinds' feet in new situations. The more often you use your faith to traverse the mountain ranges with Me the higher you will go, the more victories you'll have and the stronger you'll be.

"You were wondering if you were ready to leave the safety of where you now live to venture into dangerous domains. The beauty of the hidden place is that you never have to leave it, no matter where you go. As long as you live in life-union with Me, the sprouting Vine, the Anointed One, My words will live in power within you. You are always safe with Me" (John 15:7-8).

Standing in wonderment, I try to absorb all He has just shared. "I've never thought of it this way before, my King. Knowing you will always be traveling with me over the terrain lying ahead, takes away the fear of the future and helps me relax and enjoy the present."

"Yes. That is the way it is supposed to be." With tenderness He gathers me in His arms. My spirit soars with His to the musical dance floor of the stars where we glide in rhythm with the universe. Joy, freedom and exhilaration fill me to overflowing as I join the ultimate Dancer of the Stars.

Chapter 28

THE HIDDEN REALM

Look deep inside and you will
find

A realm unseen, existing in
between

This earth below and the one
above...

This natural realm and the realm
of love.

Your position in Christ you there
can take

And the grip of the enemy you
will break—

The grip of fear, of lack

*The grip of stress, the pain
attack.*

*The unseen realm is outside of
time.*

*The ticking of the clock will not
bind.*

*You are free to explore without
constraint,*

*Lack of strength will not be your
complaint.*

*Go where you have not gone
before,*

Dare to move, stir up, restore.

The realm inside will beckon you,

*The door will open...go through,
go through.*

Chapter 29

THE WORLD IS BRIGHT WITH LOVE

Our senses are sharpened by love:

The sight of snow sparkled
diamonds

The sound of tiny, tinkling bells

The taste of a shared mulberry
sundae

The scent of fragrant florals

The touch of a warm embrace.

The world rises in expectation to
greet us.

We rise in buoyant hope to love
and live again.

Chapter 29

THE MAKEOVER

The warm ten a.m. sunshine soothes away the morning chill on the east side of the old but comfortable sunroom. I sit there relaxing, intrigued by the songs of the robins.

All at once there is a noticeable fluctuation in the spiritual atmosphere. The Shepherd has recognized danger and at once is at my side, wrapping me in His presence (Ps. 7:10).

I sense something inside me is desperately wrong. Without warning an unexpected cry escapes my lips. "Help me, Jesus" (Matt. 15:24).

Flood gates open inside me. Trauma gushes out—a torrent of tears, fears and cries. As it pours forth, I quickly funnel it over into the hands of Christ, the Forgiver, even as His fabric of love tightens around me (Col.2:2).

I release to Him the high stress of a past incident. I had looked out the living room window as my husband's tractor went backward into the steep, water filled ditch outside the gate. I watched in horror as it ended up sideways, precariously close to tipping. Only the edge of the bucket kept it upright. One abrupt move could have spelled death. A panic-driven thirty minutes followed. The Lord sent kind neighbors over the hill at just the right time. They brought another tractor to anchor ours and move my husband to safety.

A few years ago, I slipped on the ice as I rounded the corner of my neighbors' house. My right shoulder was smashed. I lay screaming for help in the dead of winter. *Would anyone find me before morning?* But my cries were heard, and a thoughtful Schwan's driver even stopped to help my friends get me back on my feet.

Other traumatic memories tumble out, bursting from their hiding places in that dark inner room of my heart. I relived my husband's blackouts and the oxygen deprivation that led to his spinal cord injury and over fourteen years of near confinement in a wheelchair.

The Shepherd's arm around my shoulder, however, reminds me "every detail of our lives is continually woven together to fit into God's perfect plan of bringing good into our lives" (Rom. 8:28).

During the hard times I felt as though He had uprooted and scattered the puzzle pieces of my life. Now they fall back onto the table of my mind, and I see His picture taking shape. His picture. Not mine. Not the way I thought it would look. It has a grander scope than I could ever imagine. I see the mountains, valleys and dark places forming a mosaic of beauty lit by the light above. It is a breathtaking image of what has been and the hint of what is yet to be.

My thoughts return to the present, and I realize that today the doors of my soul gave way under the pressure of past fears and trauma. My will had slammed those doors shut to protect myself from any further pain. Today with His help those doorways were thrown wide open, allowing all the toxic contents to spill out.

Jesus says, "You know, it took a lot of will power and energy to hold shut those doors, to keep hidden all that fear, blame and self-hate. It drained your physical vigor and your health. But now there is no longer any 'accusing voice of condemnation against those who are joined in life-union with Jesus, the Anointed One'" (Rom. 8:1).

I turn to face the One at my side. "You are the Healer (Ps. 41:4). I want to release all my past hurts into Your hands. Take them. I don't want to be burdened with them anymore. Forgive me for holding on to those harmful emotions. Forgive me for setting my will against Yours, struggling to keep hidden what You wanted revealed and healed. Wash through this room of my heart with Your river of forgiveness. Cleanse it. Now that the darkness is exposed, come and fill it with Your light, with the over-flow of You…only You, my King" (Col. 2:9-10).

The change within me is immediate. I feel as though I have experienced a dramatic shift of some kind. His steady gaze remains on me while His smile slowly widens into a grin.

"You sense the difference, but would you like to see the actual makeover that's just occurred in that room?"

"Of course, Lord." I'm surprised, never dreaming such a thing could happen.

His words had spread a heavenly warmth throughout my heart, bringing peace beyond my human understanding (Phil. 4:7). I see the pure, dazzling light of His splendor filling the area (Song of Sg. 5:10).

"From now on this room in your heart will be your inner retreat. It will be known as the sunroom" (Ps. 90:14).

Three of the walls have been replaced with shimmering glass. Soft sunflower pillows accent the bright yellow and lime green wicker furniture. An array of exotic plants is scattered about. Clematis vines cling to trellises on the knotty pine wall. Angels sing softly in the background. He has turned this former monument to trauma into a place of rest and safety, a work of art—so beautiful and bright (Song of Sg. 5:14).

I am captivated by His tender, loving care and overwhelmed by His goodness (Ps. 23:6). His words release liquid myrrh to flow through my veins (Song of Sg. 5:13) and liquid fire to pour from my heart. Together they grow as I bend low in humble adoration and praise.

Chapter 29

THE INVITATION

*You know not inside from
outside,*

Top from bottom,

Right side from left side.

*But I AM inside and outside of
you.*

*In Me you live, move and have
your being.*

*Yet...you lack the concept of
seeing*

The vastness of My being

And your life's deeper meaning.

*In the sunrise you see My
painting,*

*In the distance you see My
drawing.*

*In the silence you hear My
calling,*

*In your belly you know My
dwelling.*

I know you inside and outside.

I made you top to bottom.

I read you right side to left side.

*Now...come know Me from inside
to outside.*

Chapter 30

THE LIVING SOURCE

What is this you have done?

You have removed yourself from
your Source.

You have neglected your true
Strength.

You have forgotten the law of
supply and demand.

Your demand upon the strength
of self has failed.

Your supply has been depleted.

There is none left.

Zip...

Zero...

Nada.

Come, sit in the silence and call My Name.

Come to the living Vine.

Be refreshed.

Be renewed.

Be replenished.

I Am your ever sufficient supply.

Chapter 30

THE WAY OF FRUITFULNESS

Streaming through the lace curtained window, the bright morning sun touches my cheek and bestirs my slumbering mind into awareness. Cheerful beams of light illuminate my warm, cozy bedroom. My mood, however, stands in stark contrast. I lie in bed this morning with a frown furrowing my forehead.

I feel out of sync, so strangely dead, as though cocooned in nothingness…barrenness. I want only to slip away into obscurity. This is not at all like me.

"Lord, I've come so far with You in the hidden place. You've been teaching me how to live. What's wrong with me this morning? Why the hopelessness? This is not living. It's just existing. Unless Your presence goes before me, I cannot even move from here" (Ex. 33:15-16 NIV).

The voice of the Master comes clearly into my thoughts. "Get up" (Acts 12:7 RSV).

That's the last thing I am inclined to do. At the same time, I'm afraid if I don't make the effort to fight my way out of this, that door of opportunity could forever be closed. It takes every ounce of my energy to sit up and swing my legs over the edge of the bed. My body seems to have gained fifty pounds overnight.

Sensation begins draining from my lower body, being replaced with numbness. I cry out to Him again, "Help me, Lord."

As I make the effort to stand on my wooden legs, He strengthens my weak knees (Heb. 12:12), and I wend my way toward the kitchen. On the way, He sparks in my memory words I had heard the night before. Making it as far as a chair, I slump into it and pull toward me the Bible on the table. Skimming through it, I find chapter 15, verse 5 in the book of John.

Glancing up, I see Him come to sit across the table from me. As usual, He has heard my intense yearning and crying out for Him, and He has come near (Song of Sg. 2:8). He doesn't interrupt but nods for me to continue. I remember to read aloud, both to Him and myself.

"I am the sprouting vine, and you're My branches. As you live in union with Me as your source, fruitfulness will stream from within you—but when you live separated from Me you are powerless."

The words cut to my heart as He explains, "You see, everything always revolves around the will. If you go off on your own, striving to live for Me in your own strength, you will become a powerless, dry, discarded branch. You won't be able to bear lasting abundant fruit because the vital, God-life in you is but a narrow rivulet. On the other hand, your total giving up of all self-effort opens wide the connection to My free-flowing supernatural sap.

"I allowed My head to be crowned with thorns, bearing for you the curse of fruitlessness in the land of your life. That is what you sensed this morning…the thorny emptiness of self. It brought you to the realization that your strength is not adequate. But that curse of barrenness is no longer yours. It legally belongs to Me. I bought all rights to it with My blood.

"Let Me take it from you. Be free."

With a sigh of relief, I release it to Him. It disappears into His nail-scarred hands as though it never existed. I look up at Him, waiting for His next words.

"The way of fruitfulness starts with your natural inclination to search for Me with all your heart, and then invite Me to blossom there. I instilled that desire in you. Next, you learn to live in Me (Song of Sg. 8:5b). But there's yet more. My words must take deep root within you and grow. You will want to be filled with My Spirit. It is He Who activates My power in you and brings the fruitfulness you desire. He allows My words to flow from you with boldness. You will be a courageous witness to My love by healing the sick, calling forth new limbs and even raising the dead. You will be a

part of the adventure of pressing into the works I
have for you" (John 14:12).

The Holy Spirit once more infuses me with
strength, and I know He will be my help in any
situation (Is. 41:10 RSV). Joy bells ring in my spirit
and light my face with a smile. I know my life is
beginning anew and all is right with the world.

I can hardly wait.

Chapter 30

FINISH STRONG

Arise within me, Spirit strong,
Help this weary soul along.
Soon will come the time to rise,
Those with You will win the
prize.

Do not forsake My Word and
Truth.
Then, with time, will come forth
fruit.
Take My hand and come along,
Together we will finish strong.

Chapter 31

ETERNITY

Father,

You have placed eternity in our
hearts

So that love can lead us home...

Back into the light from which
once we were honed.

May the longing for heaven
draw us home...

To You.

Chapter 31

THE LONGING FOR HOME

In the stillness of the warm summer evening I sit, chin in hands, on the bottom veranda step near the garden. A star-studded sky brightens the heavens, but within is an inexplicable homesickness.

I think back to a similar scene years ago when I had just moved to the outskirts of Minneapolis. I was miles away from both family and friends. I felt isolated and alone with an inner emptiness crying out for filling. Then, just as now, the loneliness within acknowledged, *"This world is not my home."*

The silence deepens under the soft light of the stars. All at once I become aware of the One sitting beside me, sharing the quietness. After a time, He speaks, reading my thoughts.

"I too was once alone in the darkness of the night, far from home and family…alone in a garden with only sleeping friends. I too felt the same emptiness. But the difference is this. Now you have Me at your side—a high priest who sympathizes with your weakness and understands your humanity. Come into My heart's room. Love is there enthroned, and you'll receive mercy's kiss and the grace you so need to strengthen you" (Heb. 4: 14-16).

I take the hand of the Prince of Peace, and my spirit enters in to sit beside Him in the comforting rest and stillness of His heart.

He continues to share with me, "When you abide here and move in My authority, peace and love, the enemy is stilled before you. Loneliness must bow. Self-accusation is silenced, and self-pity melts in My presence."

A world of wonder expands within me as I listen.

The enthusiasm ringing in His voice penetrates the night air.

"I am bringing again to the forefront the most powerful weapon in My armory, the weapon of love. Who would have thought? It was My love that broke open the doors of death, hell and the grave; but it has been many years since all My people have experienced and walked in the fullness of My love."

He leans in closer, unveiling His plan.

"The time to draw near is now, no more lingering, no more doubting. Demonstrate My love to others. As you do, peace will expand within you until we are joined as one (John 17:21). Then, we can operate from a place of victory. I, the God of peace, will soon crush enemy plans under your feet (Rom. 16:20 RSV). As you position yourself beside

Me in heavenly places, you will rule. You will see with My eyes; you will rest in Me, and we will laugh at the enemy (Ps. 2:4). All creation has been waiting for your unveiling as one of My children.

"Now let us go to the throne room of our Father who loves us."

With those words He proceeds in spirit ahead of me through the veil of the temple and into the Holy of Holies. The glory, colors and worship there all dim into the background, as I am drawn with Him into the presence of the Father (John 14:6). With eagerness Father bends over to lift me, His little one, up close to Himself. In child-like innocence my arms go around His neck and grab hold of His hair. I find in my grasp the most heavenly blend of silky wool-like hair, pure and luxurious beyond all earthly imagination—the hair of my Father. Surprise lights up my face while thoughts rush through my mind.

"No wonder He knows exactly how many hairs are on my head (Matt. 10:30). Hair is important to Him. Being made in His image, everything about me is important to Him. My Daddy God loves me! He loves me!"

I am thrilled to know I have finally found my way back home. My whole life has been a journey back to the beginning, to my Creator.

Overflowing love bursts from my heart as it joins to beat in rhythm with His. Tears of joy and relief stream down my face. I realize I've just been given a taste of my ultimate home. As Father sets me back on my feet, I again grasp the hand of my Savior. My homesickness is a thing of the past. Before we retrace our steps back to the hidden place, I turn my head to smile at Father. He smiles back at me, delight in His eyes. Now, knowing the way here with Jesus (John 14:6), I will be back to visit soon and often until my earthly journey is complete.

Chapter 31

HOME

I release you, O my heart,
into the stillness,
the deepness,
the safety of the heart of
God...
draped with the tapestry
of warmth,
richness,
and peace—
deeper, deeper still into the
depths
of the tranquility

of unfathomable peace,

into the very depths of the love of God.

Home at last.

Rest, O my heart.

Rest.

Ephesians 3:17

Chapter 32

THE HOLY ABODE

I am alone in the desert place
Withdrawn from the earthly
race.

The pace has slowed
To enter Your most holy
abode.

I now can clearly see therein
The cherubim, the
seraphim...and Him
In the light, oh, so bright.
My love it does reignite.

Within this place I long to
dwell

As a flame in the breeze to
swell—

A blue flame in the presence
of Him

Who delivered my soul from
sin.

In the Holy of Holies

Forever,

Ever

And ever.

Chapter 32

THE MIGHTY FLAME

Later that week, He finds me sitting on a stone bench in the garden. Clear bright stars adorn the luminous sky, and a full moon spreads its golden light above us. The scent of cherry blossoms drifts through the air. It's a perfect spot to ponder the day's events.

"May I join you?" He takes His place beside me, and we sit in the stillness of time, enjoying the serenity of the night.

"You have been in the desert a good portion of your life, but now you are coming up and out (Song of Sg. 8:5a). Your dying to self has severed the tie to this life. It has been a time of learning that without me you can do nothing. You have begun reaching out quickly for My hand when you fall. You realize that leaning on Me is not weakness, but the way to survive and thrive.

"You have dropped all pretense of flirting around the edges with Me—of coming close but not remaining, of coming to Me on your own terms and at your own convenience. You are now yearning for a constant abiding relationship that will remain when all else fails. You're ready for a commitment—you in Me and My steady loving presence in you.

"I do give Myself to you. I pour My Spirit into you, My Bride, My loved one. You are now Mine, and I am yours. 'Fasten Me upon your heart as a seal of fire forevermore. This living, consuming flame will seal you as My prisoner of love'" (Song of Sg.8:6a).

"Lord," I interrupt, "that sounds kind of scary. I don't know if I want to be a prisoner again. I want to remain free."

"Oh, but you are free. There is always a choice. You can choose to be captivated by self or surrounded by Love. Self is a cruel master. You will die trying to please self."

His lips close together for a second and a cloud of memories seems to pass over His eyes before He blinks them away. "I became a willing prisoner of death so that you could be free to choose."

A mighty change sweeps through my now broken heart, removing the last vestiges of self. The same cheeks that were a few short hours ago lit by sunshine now become riverbeds for tears of sorrow. They drop on His hands which now hold mine.

"Forgive me, my Savior, for not understanding earlier. Forgive me for turning away from You without even realizing it."

As He gazes at me under the starry sky, His eyes are brimming with fiery love. He seems to see right through me—reading my heart line by line (Ps. 139:4). "As I once asked Peter, I ask you, 'Do you burn with love for Me? Is it a love that is passionate, kindling a holy flame in your heart'" (John 21:15 footnote)?

"I want to, Lord. Help me. Set my lukewarm heart on fire."

His answer arises from deep within.

"My passion is stronger than the chains of death and the grave, all-consuming as the very flashes of fire from the burning heart of God. Place this fierce, unrelenting fire over your entire being. Rivers of pain and persecution will never extinguish this flame. Endless floods will be unable to quench this raging fire that burns within you. Everything will be consumed. It will stop at nothing as you yield everything to this furious fire until it won't seem to you like a sacrifice anymore" (Song of Sg. 8:6-7).

My now flaming heart melts into a warm pool of love as I respond, "I yield, my King. I take You, the Mighty Flame of the hidden place, to be my dwelling forevermore."

And all is well with my soul.

Chapter 32

THE BRIDEGROOM

"I have betrothed you. You are mine.

Come into the bridal chamber of time.

Open wide the gates of your being,

Your hunger and thirst bring Me in.

I wait for you.

Cover Me...

With the love that is you.

Be still.

Absorb My peace, My love, My essence.

Release all resistance.

Let Me fan into blazing fire the smoldering

embers of your heart.

Let Me fill you to overflowing with My oil,

Let it ooze from your pores…My joy, My life, My scent.

Be not hesitant.

Come.

Chapter 33

THE PATH

Within the hidden place, you know,

is a path you can choose to go.

With Holy Spirit's assistance,

you'll enter the peace of no resistance.

It is the path of living trust,

and only those who let go

move into the Spirit's flow.

Chapter 33

THE PURITY OF INNOCENCE

The night stars twinkled in my heart with the wonder of the knowledge of the glory of God (II Cor. 4:6). I kept alive the memories of the prior hours. I pondered them over and over.

Even in a dream I heard myself speaking, *"I need you, Lord. I don't want to be apart from You anymore. I want to be one with You all the time, no more separation."*

"But your heart is dark," is His soft reply.

"Then change it, Lord. Change it. I can't."

At the crack of dawn, with evening shadows still lingering, I hear His voice.

"Come. It's time. Last night the fire of love burned. Today the fire of purity burns."

"What?" My still sleepy brain struggles to wrap itself around His words.

"Make yourself ready and then come with Me."

My thoughts are confounded. *"What is this fire?"* My natural mind does not understand.

However, I have learned to trust Him; I know He wants only my best. As soon as I am ready, I slip my hand into His (James 1:17). At once my hesitancy disappears, and we head down the valley beyond the fields and then upward again. Soon we near the mountains which before I had only seen in the distance (Song of Sg. 4:6).

I see His face set, eyes focused on what is directly ahead. His steps are resolute, as though moved by an unshakeable purpose.

After a while we come to a resting spot and just sit together. There He shares, "The time has come for your entering into a deeper walk with Me…a baptism of fire" (Luke 3:16 footnote).

My mind puzzles over His words.

We follow a rocky, narrow path up to an altar crafted by the Maker Himself. The top lays covered with heavy, packed dirt.

With widened eyes I stand looking at it. I realize this place is a necessary stage of my growth, the entrance leading to the release of my destiny. Such a sense of purpose settles over me that I am drawn to willingly position myself on the altar. With my surrender of self, I trust the Shepherd. I am not afraid. I know He loves me. No matter what happens, His plan for me is only good (Jer. 29:11 RSV).

Lying down, I brush aside the veil that covers my heart of stone. Inside, I see the result of the disease of sin…rottenness to the core. I turn my head, unable to look at the ugliness and decay. The putrid stench turns my stomach. I know I can only be restored by His purifying fire. I find my will in total agreement with His. What He wants for me, I will not strain against (Acts 26:14).

Silvery streams of sparkling light begin settling into my heart as I lie still in His presence. With the eyes of my spirit, I see flaming particles of light absorbing the darkness bit by bit. The fire from heaven carries healing in its wings and covers me in its glory.

I feel no pain, but I can sense my heart changing with each burning away of a sin stain. I feel more and more at rest until I am loosed from the bonds of time and slip into a deep sleep where all is peace.

I know not how long I've lain here under His watchful care, but I am awakened by the shining light of His presence. Looking up, I notice Him nod with sweet anticipation in the direction of my heart. I glance down to see all traces of darkness gone (I John 2:8). It is transparent and pure. I see only pulsating particles of sparkling, white light and a blue flame of love burning in the clear oil of His anointing. Gazing in wonder at it all, I give thanks for the mighty transformation brought about by the fire of God.

No longer on the altar, my body now lies on the thick green grass of the sun-warmed earth. Still waters flow beside me. I feel healthy and alive in His presence. *"Is this what it was like for Adam the*

Lying there, I absorb the beauty of what has always been my inheritance (Acts 26:18). I am overflowing with the richness of Him. He is my hidden place, my security and my provider of every good and perfect gift (James 1:17). In the purity of innocence, I am united in spirit with Him. He will always be my springboard into the unknown adventures lying ahead.

Time is hushed as we radiate joy in the richness of the moment. As He helps me to my feet, His nearness brings recognition that this is now the beginning of what life was originally meant to be (Col. 3:10). We can now venture forward together as broken bread and poured out wine into the dawn of a new day. A universe awaits, and there are still miles to go before I sleep.

Chapter 33

EXPANSION

...the ever-expanding brilliant
light of My presence,

taking you from where you are
to Who I am...

pushing out the darkness,

filling the emptiness,

breaking through the confines of
your earthly flesh,

surging into the atmosphere
surrounding you,

engulfing all in all

and sweeping you up into the
dominion

of light

to the King of Kings and the
Lord of Lords

forever and ever.

Live in the light.

Walk in the light.

Be the light.

THE MYSTERY

I want to show you a mystery
great and true,
an open door for you
to peek through.
The colors are purple and blue,
a royal tapestry true
—it is My essence—
peeking through.
I look at you and see you
through and through.
I begin to change you through
and through
until when you look at you,
you see Me
peeking through.

II Cor. 3:18

EPILOGUE

My intentions for this book were to create in each reader both an awareness of the hidden place and a deep thirst to drink of Jesus' eternal well of life.

I have given you glimpses into my own personal journey, but I believe the hidden place will look different to each of you. We are all vital parts of the body of believers and relate uniquely to the King of Love. What looks and feels like love to one may not necessarily fulfill that need in another. Yet, we individually are only complete once we are in Him, the Anointed One (Col. 2:9-10).

It is vitally important that we each, as members of the Bride of Christ, be eager to enter our own place in Him—to receive His love and acceptance and to delight in Him.

"Come, says the Holy Spirit and the Bride *in divine duet.* Let everyone who hears *this duet* join them in saying, "Come." Let everyone gripped with *spiritual* thirst say, "Come." And let everyone who craves the gift of living water come and drink it freely. *"It is my gift to you!* Come" (Rev. 22:17).

ABOUT THE AUTHOR

Connie Victoria Volk has always claimed the starry, wide-open country of the Dakotas as her home.

After graduating from Northern State College in Aberdeen, SD, she taught English and Spanish in various mid-western schools. After the death of her husband and mother, she pursued her passion for writing and her family's love of painting.

She is blessed with two wonderful daughters and three grandchildren.

She was one of the first members of the Healing Rooms of the Northern Plains in Bismarck, ND and is a Director of the Healing Room Kids.

COPYRIGHT

Cover design by Solutions Website Design. Adapted from a painting by the author.